MAKING A BENT SHAFT LAMINATED CANOE PADDLE

INSTRUCTIONS FOR THE DIY PADDLE MAKER

JEFF BACH

QUIETWATER MEDIA, LLC.
STOUGHTON, WI., USA

Jeff Bach/Quietwater Media, llc.
Stoughton, WI., USA 53589
www.quietwaterpaddles.com

Ordering Information:
Special discounts are available for paddling/canoe clubs. For details, contact the author at paddle@quietwaterpaddles.com.

Contents

Other Books and DVDs by Jeff Bach

DVD Making a Bent Shaft Laminated Canoe Paddle

Making a Bent Shaft Laminated Paddleboard Paddle

DVD Making a Bent Shaft Laminated Paddleboard Paddle

Making a Straight Shaft Laminated Canoe Paddle

DVD Making a Straight Shaft Laminated Canoe Paddle

related DVDs from quietwater films

paddling a solo canoe
paddling a tandem canoe
paddling the recreational kayak
inland waters kayak fishing with Jimbo Meador
gulf coast kayak fishing with Jimbo Meador

Paddling and water have been life long companions for me. Some of my biggest joys have been watching my kids paddling boats and playing around with them. This book is dedicated to those paddlers that pass on their love of paddling and the outdoors, and hopefully paddle making, to the next generation of paddlers.

Figure 1: A Future Paddler in All Her Paddling Glory

"What nobody tells people who are beginners – and I really wish someone had told this to me . . . is that all of us who do creative work, we get into it because we have good taste. But there is this gap. For the first couple years you make stuff, and it's just not that good. It's trying to be good, it has potential, but it's not. But your taste, the thing that got you into the game, is still killer. And your taste is why your work disappoints you. A lot of people never get past this phase. They quit. Most people I know who do interesting, creative work went through years of this. We know our work doesn't have this special thing that we want it to have. We all go through this. And if you are just starting out or you are still in this phase, you gotta know it's normal and the most important thing you can do is do a lot of work. Put yourself on a deadline so that every week you will finish one story. It is only by going through a volume of work that you will close that gap, and your work will be as good as your ambitions. And I took longer to figure out how to do this than anyone I've ever met. It's gonna take awhile. It's normal to take awhile. You've just gotta fight your way through."

—IRA GLASS

[1]

Introduction

Bent shaft, laminated, wood canoe paddles made by hand with hand tools. Just wanted to make the subject of this book clear in the first line. Sorry it's not a complete sentence.

Woodworking is an experiential kind of thing. You need to do it in order to understand it and acquire the skills and perspective and trickery you need to turn out a finished product. Reading a book is only the start, you must then follow up by doing the work.

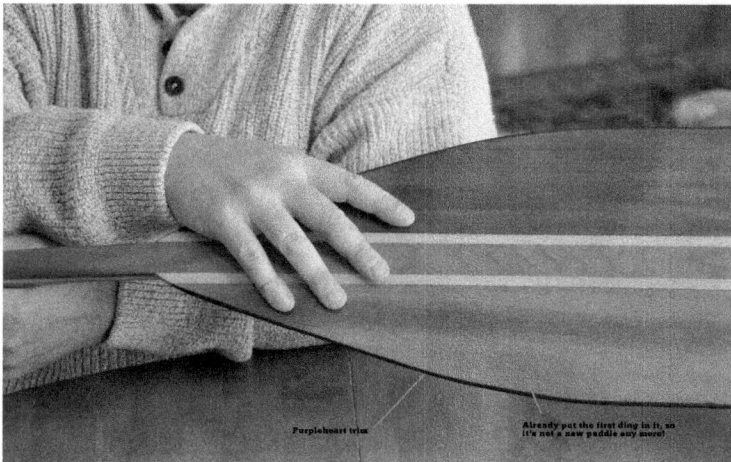

Purpleheart trim   Already put the first ding in it, so it's not a new paddle any more!

Figure 2: Here's What You are After - a Paddle Made by You!

Like so many other experiential things (e.g. riding a bike), the first few times you fall down. But the falling is very instructional. You learn what to do and what not do for the next time. This is woodworking as well. You have to experience the tools and how wood reacts. Importantly, you learn to control the feeling of just "wanting to be done". You learn to enjoy the journey and not just rush to get to the destination.

As clichéd as that may read, I think it is true. It's not just about the wood and the tools, it is about being patient and not overdoing things, letting the tools do the work and not overpowering them with too much muscle. Most wood is fairly easy to work, especially when you have ripped it into thin narrow strips. It yields easily to sandpaper and spokeshave and especially block plane. So go easy until you know what you and the tools are capable of doing to wood. Because, as you will no doubt discover, especially with the first paddle....

It is easy to take the wood off and nearly impossible to put it back on!

There's two versions of this book. The other version is an instruction manual in a paddle making kit that quietwater paddles sells. I started with a kit that includes an assembled form and all of the wood pieces already pre-cut.

In an instruction manual everything is already decided and planned out and included in the kit. The paddle form and the shaft strips being obvious examples. The paddle maker would then need ONLY hand tools to make their paddles. Power tools would not be required, which is an advantage of the kit.

After doing the "no power tools required" kit, I was reminded that there are wood workers with power tools and wood working experience that also enjoy paddling. So I took the instruction manual and created another version, which is what you now have in your hand. The other big difference between the kit and this book is that with a kit you get a package with wood, fiberglass cloth and epoxy quantities that fit the amount needed for two paddles.

My thought here is that the reader of this book has the tools and the wood working perspective to work their way first through sourcing the materials and then creating the rough pieces and then making the finished paddle.

In a blatant plug for the kit (sorry), if you do not have the set up to rip long pieces of wood on a table saw or rip the three inch blade pieces, I hope you will consider buying the wood pieces from quietwater. They're here ready to use, in both cedar and aspen, no ripping necessary.

IT'S IN YOUR HEAD

Woodworking with your hands is a vanishing art. I love how hand-powered hand tools feel. I love how they sound. This is a great analog effort in our increasingly digital world. Paddle projects more or less force you to go slow and engage with your hands and your eye. There are very few flat surfaces on a paddle. Measuring anything is hard to do. The world increasingly wants things to be quantitative. Making a paddle reminds us of the qualitative world, where you have to go by "feel". Paddle making is a "good enough" world. There is no measurement to aim for. Pick your paddle up in your hands. That is how you determine the final fit and feel. When it is "good enough" for your hands and eyes, it is done!

More than tools or the wood, it's been my observation, both of myself and of watching others, that people get caught up in precisely following directions, thinking that things must be exact, and that crushing force must be used when clamping and holding. This book is not a set of precise directions. Please consider the steps I work through as "guidelines", simply based on my paddle making experience. No worries if you want to do things a bit different. Use power tools or other methods if you think they will do what you want. Stop and think your diversion through, reread the prior few steps and maybe scan the next few steps. After doing so, if you think your departure still works then go for it. Use the guidelines as much as you want.

Most things do not have to be "exact". Paddle making is closer to an art than a science. Think qualitative not quantitative. Think through your steps, maybe even rehearse them, but measuring down to the 0.01 inch is going too far. Paddle making is NOT an exact anything. It is approximating and "close enough". Recognize our tendency to overdo things including measuring everything we can. Bend down and put your eye against the roughed in shaft and check it for straightness. No tools are needed for that. Go primitive. Trust your eye.

Mixing the epoxy used in joining the wood pieces and in fiberglassing the blade requires a bit of care. Nothing approaching rocket science though, if you can use a measuring cup in a kitchen you can mix the resin and hardener that together make up epoxy.

Finally, crushing force is **NOT NEEDED** for anything in this project. Making a paddle can be done with the strength in your fingers and hands. Compression bars can be gently compressed, with just a couple gentle turns of the wing nuts once contact is made. A really tight compression bar is only going to squeeze all the epoxy out of the joint. No need for that. You want the epoxy in the join, not dribbling down the side of the wood stack.

When using tools, think two or three fingers, not pressing the tool down into the wood with the strength in both arms. Sandpaper in particular works better when the downward force is light.

Most people are anxious to get their paddle completed. So they hurry. Most wood is fairly soft and easy to remove. Any wood is hard to add back on. So do your best to **leisurely** enjoy paddle making. Avoid being in a hurry to get something done. That is when you accidentally remove too much wood, thus making yourself sick over the hastily done damage you did to your future paddle. Think about each pull (or push) of your spokeshave, block plane, or cabinet scraper. Go slowly through the process. Hurrying is the easiest way to make a mistake. **Remember - it's easy to take the wood off. It's hard to put the wood back on.** This one mental concept has cost me more lost time, materials and paddles than anything else.

There's a certain amount of "Zen" to making anything with wood including a bent shaft laminated paddle. Think relaxed tool movements with the strength of fingers and hands, not huge crushing arms and body blows. Whenever you can, hold the paddle in your hands. Test the fit. Does the shaft fit the shape of your lower hand grip? Does the handle fit the shape of your upper hand grip? Switch hands. Does it feel as good with your off hand as it does with your strong hand?

The bend in the shaft is another area of concern. Many first time paddle makers try and completely "squish" (a technical term there) the wood in the bend all the way down to the form, especially with the first piece. It will not happen. It can't happen. This is a bend not a corner. There is going to be a gap at the apex of the bend, under the wood and above the form. Jump ahead to Figure 10 to see what I mean. Remember, the more pressure you apply, the more epoxy you are going to squeeze out of the joint. That epoxy is the strength. You want it in the joint, not dribbling down the side of the stack. "Close enough" is the phrase that hopefully comes to mind. I look for that gap below the bend apex to be about one quarter of an inch or so.

TIME AND SPACE

Paddle making, at least the way I do it and consequently how this book is written tends to be in steps. Bent shaft laminated paddles are incrementally completed, not all built in one session. So try and avoid telling your significant other that this is a one day project. Be sure and have space where you can leave your stuff set out. The shaft strips are done one join one at a time. Position, apply epoxy, add the next piece, compress a bit, check alignment, and let dry. About twenty minutes of work at a time, followed by several hours of curing. By the way, the blade pieces and the handle can be worked on separately while the shaft joinery is drying.

Even though you do need a bit of space to work, an unexpected benefit of using the form is that you can do your work on it and then pick it up and move it out of the way while the epoxy is drying. So you can make a kitchen counter or table top paddle and still use both as part of the kitchen! The form is portable and can be moved. In my experience with my wife of 20+ years, this is a nice feature!

TOOLS

I love my spokeshave. It feels good as you pull it along the shaft. It even sounds good. Spokeshaves are finesse tools. Or at least they should be used as if they are finesse tools. Mostly fingers and hands. Just a little bit of arms. The blade in a spokeshave is recessed up into the throat plate far enough that digging in and following the grain is hard to do. Little of the blade is exposed with a spokeshave, so I tend to consider it one of the safer tools.

Figure 3: Spokeshave, Block Plane, and Cabinet Scrapers, Big Three Paddle Making Tools

Cabinet scrapers are my next favorite tool. Pushing and pulling this basic square piece of metal is another wood working pleasure. Scrapers work really well for removing dried epoxy, especially along the join lines of the blade pieces. Scrapers also work quite well after you have run a block plane over the shaft joins and knocked off the bigger peaks.

A block plane can be handy at times. It can remove wood much faster than a spokeshave or scraper, but that must be balanced with the increased ease of the plane "digging" into the wood as it follows the grain. This can lead to a nasty looking gash in the wood or a bigger gouge than you were looking to make. Practice with this tool first and make sure the blade is set to remove the thinnest possible shaving that you can set it for.

Finishing the surfaces is an important part of the paddle project. Scrapers, microplanes, sanding blocks, sandpaper, and even a surform are some of the basic tools that have a place in paddle making. The thing with sandpaper is following the progression of grits. For example, 100 grit works wonders. Especially on cedar. Almost too much. But the 100 grit leaves behind obvious scratch lines, that will be painfully clear under epoxy or varnish. So you need to follow the 100 grit with the 120 grit, then the 150, maybe the 180, and even a 220 grit if you really want a smooth finish. Making too big of a jump from the first grit to the next does a poor job removing the underlying scratch marks. Be patient and follow the progression. Keep in mind that once you have the fiberglass on the blade, you will be able to sand that surface as well. Prior to applying the fiberglass and epoxy on the blade I generally just use 150 grit on the blade pieces. The fiberglass surface (which is the final finished surface) I go all the way to 220 grit after the first coating.

For paddle making, I think a drawknife is too much. It's too easy to accidentally remove too much wood with a drawknife. I've also found that a drawknife tends to follow the grain too easily, so it can really dig in. A drawknife has a larger exposed blade, so there's more of a safety issue with that tool.

Whether you decide to go from scratch or maybe buy some wood pieces or a form from quietwater, I hope you enjoy the experience!

The Paddle Form

It's been my experience in paddle making that keeping the shaft pieces aligned during assembly and having an easy way to do that is an important part of the paddle making process. An ability to test fit pieces while dry, which usually requires adding and removing pieces and making marks that allow exact repositioning of pieces is another piece of shaft assembly. Working with a bend in the midst of it all also adds another layer of complexity.

In the rest of the woodworking world, similar functions are accomplished with jigs. Paddle making is no different. The jig I use and also sell (hint hint), I call a paddle form. Of course I am biased when I write this, but buying a paddle form from quietwater will save you the time and effort of buying the materials and then laying it out yourself. However, if building jigs flips your minnow, then stop reading this chapter and skip over to **Appendix 1**. There I have explained and illustrated the form. There is also a materials list for a form. Or you can buy a form that is ready to use from quietwater (last hint I promise).

THE WOOD

Boat building historically has used a select few certain woods. In some cases, the reason for a certain wood is lost in the misted obscurity of time and now people are just using it because that is what people have always done. In other cases there are sound reasons for using a certain type of wood. As far as I can tell, in my experience there are no absolutes that must be followed.

Cedar has a great strength to weight ratio, it seems to do well around water and it tolerates being bent. I also love how cedar smells when it is being worked, although that is not quite a reason to use it in a paddle. It is also available as clear, vertical grain, affordable lumber in my neck of the woods. All of which adds up to why I prefer to use cedar in my paddles. I also like poplar, which some call aspen, in part because I like the creamy color of it compared to the cedar. Neither wood is absolutely required though. For example, if you have basswood you might consider using it in lieu of the poplar. Pine can work and is probably the most widely available wood across the USA, although it can be a bit difficult to work with a spokeshave. The first set of blades I ever made were out of pine. Years later, I still have that paddle and the blade still works just fine, even though it is made from wood not associated with boat building. If that is what you have or can afford, give it a try, especially if the alternative is nothing. Personally, I do not like oak one little bit. I think it burns too easily when you are cutting it. It is also heavy. But it will work if that is what you have. Just about any wood when ripped into a long thin strip is going to be flexible and will bend when pressed down on the angle block. Do your research. Some would say that poplar might a bit stronger than basswood. It's personal too. I think poplar is a creamier white than basswood and I like that better creaminess better than the less white color of basswood. There are no absolutes and many different wood species will work just fine. Research, ask around, it's always pleasant talking wood and tools after all. It's all good!

One last note. In my years of paddling, from guiding canoe trips in the Boundary Waters to rafting on the Salmon River all the way through to now paddling on Wisconsin lakes, I have never broken a wood canoe paddle. I did break a wood oar once in a big drop on the upper Klamath in northern California. But I was a little stressed at the time. It is possible to break a paddle. Paddles are not indestructible. Once you have the form and the tools and have gone through the process once, you are set in terms of turning out additional paddles. That way if you do fall on the middle of the shaft while the ends are suspended between two rocks, or merely crunch the blade in the car door, you can repair the paddle or make yourself another one.

By the way, using the paddle like a bat and swinging at rocks, does leave some pretty healthy dings in the blade that are hard to remove.

Not that one of my kids ever did anything like that while they were bored in camp one day....

Please note that every once in awhile, a topic pops up in the middle of another topic. Rather than shoving this tangent off into an appendix, I use "**OPTION ASIDE**" to warn you that we are going to digress for a bit. "**END ASIDE**" returns you to your regularly scheduled reading.

It may seem like I skip around a bit, but that is because at times a topic that comes later in the project may also figure in to an earlier planning stage. When that occurs, I do try and bring that later piece in to that earlier planning discussion. This may seem like I'm going out of order, which is not my intent. It's just that paddle making is not the most linear process in the world.

Also, shaft, blade, and handle are covered twice. The first time through I'm trying to emphasize assembly and the second time through I'm trying to emphasize the finishing process.

[2]

Paddle Making the Leadup

THE WOOD

Wood paddles obviously need wood. Below are pictures of shaft strips, blades and handles that the author uses to make paddles. More information on wood can be found in **Appendix 2**.

Figure 4: Cedar and Aspen Shaft Strips the Author Cut

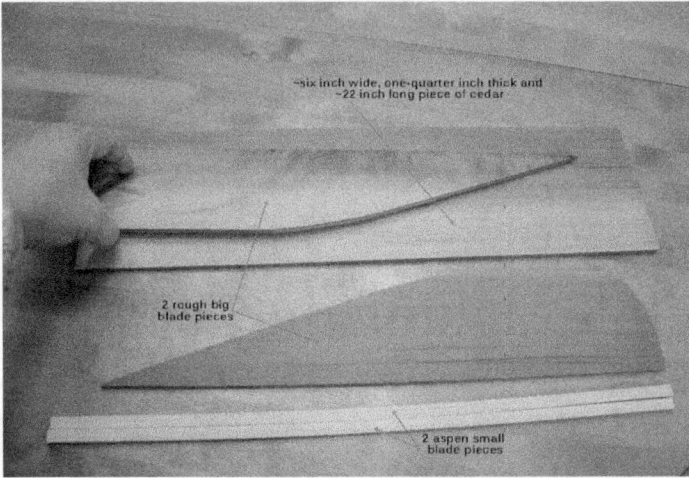

Figure 5: blade blank, and four rough blade pieces

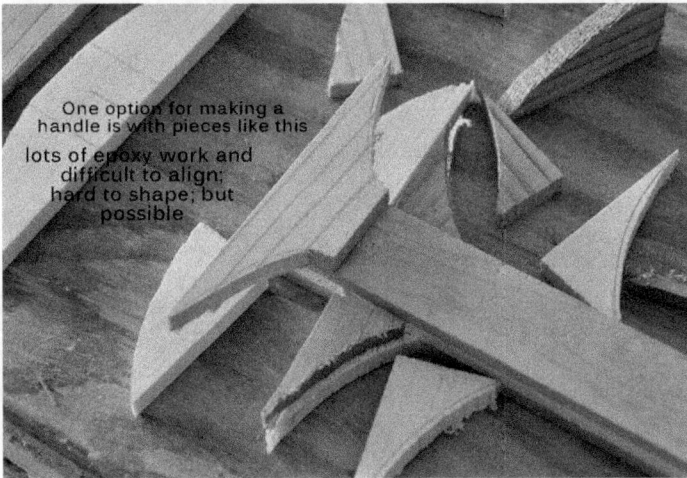

Figure 6: Pieces like this are an option for building up a handle

Figure 7: Another Style of Handle Starts Out as One Piece and is Shaped

For most people, this will be the first time they have ever tried to make a paddle. As we all know, mistakes happen, especially when it comes to doing something for the first time. So go into this expecting to have a "throwaway" first paddle and a usable second paddle. A usable first paddle is a happy bonus. Experience is truly the very best teacher when it comes to hand-powered tools!

DECIDING ON PADDLE LENGTH

Do your research and decide how long you want your paddle to be. There are plenty of resources online. Maybe you have other paddles or your friends do. Sneak a measuring tape into a store and measure the paddles that feel good as you stand in front of the rack ~~drooling~~ looking at them. It's not an exact process. But you still need a number. Inches or centimeters. No need to overdo the measuring, stick with whole numbers. Bent shaft paddles are going to be significantly shorter than straight shaft paddles.

There are many different methods, each one of which asserts that it is correct. Pick a source you like or trust and run with it. For what it is worth, I like what Darren Bush and Rutabaga[1] have to say about bent shaft paddle length. If you choose to buy a handle from quietwater, please keep in mind that the handle adds an inch to the total paddle length.

Speaking of Darren Bush, I have to put in a plug for Canoecopia at this point. Every March, Madison, WI., turns into paddling central. For three days the Alliant Energy Center turns into the country's largest paddlesports store. Lots of bent shaft paddles to look at. Darren Bush is a key cog in that event, which is put on by Rutabaga. It's like a cold destination for spring break, full of canoes and other boating gear and lots of happy people!

OPTION ASIDE-If you are agonizing about paddle length, there is another unofficial option. But don't tell anyone. Sometimes, for paddles I make for me, I like to assemble the shaft, leaving it an inch or so longer than my suspected target length. I leave the top few inches of the shaft "unepoxied" and rough the shaft into shape. I do all the blade shaping, assembling and fiberglassing but I leave the handle and shaft **UNFINISHED**. I work the handle such that I can get it seated firmly on the roughed in shaft, but still loose. It is also still in its rough shape.

Then I take this unfinished paddle out for its first paddle. I use it in real water while I am sitting in my real canoe. This gives me a chance to assess shaft length and how the handle feels. Afterward, I take this "once used" paddle back to the bench with a much better feel for overall length and how the handle feels in my hands. I shorten the shaft if needed, recut the notch (possible because the shaft pieces are still loose at the top) and then with my shaft at its now final length, I

---

[1]Www.paddlingexperts.com/sitecontent/all-things-canoe/how-to-select-a-canoe-paddle

apply (poke or push might be better words) epoxy in between the upper few inches of the shaft pieces for the final time. **END ASIDE.**

Part of feeling good when paddling is keeping your shaft as close to vertical as you can when moving it through the water. In my experience a taller (some say longer) paddle is going to make you stretch and lift more to keep the shaft vertical. You work harder because your handle hand lifts a little higher than it would with a shorter paddle. Instead of your handle hand being at chin level when you start a stroke, it might be up above your forehead. This sounds trivial but it does tire your shoulders out. After a day of working against gravity like this, you'll know it! A longer paddle also extends your joints more putting them at greater risk of injury.

Also worth considering is if this paddle is going to be for a bow paddler. If so, then a bit more length may be OK, given the constraints of bow paddling. If the paddle is going to be mainly a stern paddle, then I think shorter is better.

To me, a paddle that is too short is better than one that is too long. With a shorter paddle, you are spending less energy fighting gravity and you are not putting your joints into as much of a stretch as you do with a longer paddle. Your reach to the front will be shorter. But this still tends to be minor in almost all cases. It still feels good to paddle with a short paddle. If in doubt make your first paddle shorter. Go use it and then revise length as needed with your second paddle. **END ASIDE**

I see main three parts to building a paddle - assembly, shaping and sanding, and fiberglass and finishing. Maybe there's more if you're a detail person. But three is good for now. Some steps in the process can happen in a different order if you want. Nothing is written in stone here.

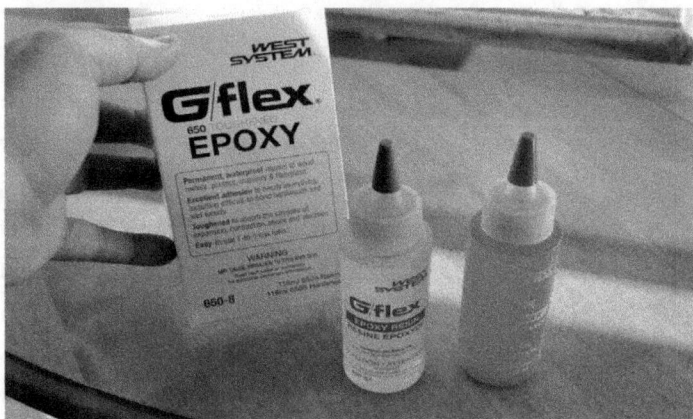

Figure 8: West Systems GFlex for wood to wood joinery

The first step, assembly, is laminating the shaft strips together with epoxy, adding the blade pieces to the shaft with epoxy, and again using epoxy to add the handle. I like West Systems GFlex for joining wood to wood. GFlex is "pretoughened" as West Systems calls it. I have used it quite often and always enjoyed the results. West Systems sells a small kit (part no. 650-8; see Figure 8) that is just the right size for two paddle projects. Lots of good epoxy brands out there, so if you trust another brand for wood to wood joining, keep at it. GFlex is what I started with. I've never felt a need to try others.

Shaping and sanding is all about tools and teasing the finished surface out of the unfinished wood. This step is patiently applying spokeshave, block plane, scrapers, micro plane, and sandpaper to the shaft, blade pieces, and handle in order to remove extra wood and bring out the paddle waiting within. This is an iterative process, meaning that you are going to be doing the same thing over and over. Remove a little wood. Hold it in both hands. Feel it. Put your eye down along the shaft - Does it look symmetrical? Is there a bulge somewhere? Remove a little more wood and look again. Repeat as needed until you are happy with the look and the fit.

Remember - it is easy to take wood off and hard to put it back on!

The final part is applying the fiberglass cloth and epoxy to the blade and then finishing. Fiberglassing is a smallish part of the project that yields big results. Only the blade receives the cloth and epoxy treatment. I have a fondness for four ounce cloth, and another soft spot for MAS epoxy when it comes to working with fiberglass cloth. MAS is easy to mix (2:1 ratio), it does not smell (at least to my nose), it dries clear and lets the color, texture, and grain of the wood show through the fiberglass. It offers ample work time but still dries nicely. Good stuff.

I like GFlex for joining wood pieces together.

I like MAS for the blade fiberglass.

Of course there are myriad other options here. Feel free to go with what you know or find in your own research.

Finishing is also smallish in nature, but can yield amazing and beautiful results, especially if patience is in plentiful supply and the correct progression of sand paper is used!

[3]

Paddle Making - the Shaft

The shaft is five pieces of wood laminated together. The simple addition of epoxy between the layers transforms weak, flexible spaghetti noodle pieces of wood into a stiff and strong paddle shaft. The shaft is bent using an angle block. It is not cut. See Appendix 1. This means that the wood remains a single whole piece, rather than being cut at angle and then rejoined like many other bent shaft paddles.

When it comes time to rip the rough pieces, I shoot for the shaft strips to be one-quarter inch thick and I set my rip fence accordingly. The quarter inch thickness works well for me with cedar and aspen when it comes to bending the shaft strips. Five strips x quarter inch gives me a shaft stack 1.25 inches thick, which I have found to yield a nice finished size that fits the average hand. If you have big hands you can increase the thickness of each strip (9/32nds or even a bit more) if you want. Just keep in mind the thicker the strip the more it will fight bending. OR you can add a sixth strip.

LAYOUT FOR SHAFT AND BLADE

The first shaft strip is the longest piece. You will be joining the bottom of this first shaft strip with the blade pieces and the top with the handle. Along with this longest shaft piece, get all of the blade pieces (e.g. two wide cedar and two narrow aspen) and lay them out on a flat surface with that first long shaft strip. Make sure the bottoms of all five pieces are even. Keep in mind that one side of this shaft strip will be part of the power face of the paddle and it might be a tad more visible. Also keep in mind that the thin aspen blade pieces are optional. I like the color contrast they provide and I like the finished width of the paddle blade when they are included. If you want a smaller blade or a paddle that is all cedar, simply do not use the aspen pieces. If you want a wider paddle blade, making the thin strips wider is the easiest way to do that.

You can of course make your own blade pieces to fit the profile of your choosing. The easiest way to do this may be to just trace around one of your existing paddle blades. Take that traced shape and transfer it to your wood piece(s). A combination of table saw and band saw will yield the two half pieces to bond on each side of the center shaft piece.

Figure 9: Marking the Main Shaft Where Blade Pieces Terminate

Turn blade and shaft pieces over a few times and see if there are combinations of grain patterns or color variations that please your eye. Keep in mind that the top side of each shaft piece is going to be covered by the other shaft strips. Juggle the pieces around and evaluate the fit and the look. Flip them over. Change sides. Make light pencil marks such that you can get the same pieces back together again facing the same way. Using marks makes it easy to place and replace pieces in their correct location. Small marks though, that you can erase or that sanding will completely remove. I stay away from Sharpies and pens as the marks are hard to remove.

Make a mark on the shaft piece where the top of the blade pieces terminate against the shaft strip. Not a big mark, but one you can see. Doesn't have to be exact.

The point of this mark is so that you know where the top of the blade pieces join the shaft. This is important because the bend of the shaft starts close to the top of the blade pieces. You have to make a design decision about how the tip ends of the blade pieces are going to fall relative to the bend in the shaft. You will use this mark as part of that decision.

The mark gives you something consistent, so if you take your shaft stack out of the form, you can put it back in the same place using the marks. Make the mark on the sides of the pieces as well. If you mark the top, remember that the next strip you add will cover the mark, so transfer the mark to the top of this new piece.

Now transfer that mark to both sides of the form. This comes in handy when you remove the shaft strips. With marks **ON BOTH SIDES** of the form it is easy to replace the shaft strips exactly where you want them in the form relative to the angle block and the apex of the bend.

Make three marks on each side of the form/shaft stack at the bottom, middle, and top. Multiple marks on both sides makes it easy to replace and re-align the pieces as you go about making your paddle. Marking both sides comes in quite handy. It is amazing how many times your hands are full and it's hard to move and you can't see the marks because they are on the other side.

Now set out the form. Pop the angle block into place if you have not done so already. Lay that first shaft strip, the one you just made the mark on, in the form with the bottom 18 inches or so laying on the angle block. Aim for the mark you made on the shaft strip to line up with the bottom of the form. Push the piece down between the alignment blocks that are spaced along the form. You can loosen the alignment bars a bit if the fit is too tight. Spend some time flexing this first piece down into its "bend". Pay attention to the apex of the curve, which is right where the angle block meets the form. It is important to recognize that no matter how hard you crush this down there is always going to be a gap under the apex of the curve. See Figure 10.

GENTLY press down with your fingers on top of this first piece and get a feel for how much force you need to get this first piece to make the bend. This shape is a BEND NOT A SHARP CORNER. This is more organic than geometric. Remember that Zen thing and put your latent engineering tendencies to the side. **Do not try and force the wood into a corner**. The inside of the bend (the top) is being compressed. The outside (the bottom) is getting stretched. The pieces will need to adjust and slip a bit as you bend them. The wood has to adjust to that curve. Take your time here. Play with this piece and get a feel for how the wood behaves. There's no rush. Wood is infinitely different. Don't force anything. Be patient. Sometimes it will behave

perfectly. Sometimes the wood will just snap. Sometimes you'll get a bit of a warning. So go easy the first few times until you have a feel for how your wood piece is behaving.

Once you have a "feel" for how this first strip behaves, tighten down the first compression bar on top of it until the bend stays in place.

Figure 10: Gap at the Bend Will Always Be There

There will always be a gap under this first piece right where the angle block meets the form. THIS GAP IS OK and is part of the process. Once the compression block is tightened down (later on), the gap should be about one quarter inch. For me, I can stick the sharp end of a pencil a little ways under the bend, but the whole pencil should not be able to slide under the bend. Here at the start finger pressure is what you need.

Hold the blade piece(s) next to that shaft strip. The alignment bar(s) holding the angle block may be in the way for this. You can unscrew and remove the bars if you want to make holding the blade piece against the shaft piece easier.

Find the mark you made earlier on the shaft piece. Spend the next several minutes adjusting the shaft strip **UP or DOWN** on the angle block until there is enough of it laying on the block to match up with the length of the blade. If you want the blade to be straight and flat, then make sure that the mark you made is sufficiently below the beginning of the bend. If you want the top of the blade pieces to have a bit of a bend then adjust accordingly.

Remember this is wood. It's organic with a mind of its own. If this is the first time you have done something like this, keep your expectations flexible. You may end up with a bit of a bend at the top of the blade whether you planned it or not. As with most things, you'll have options and a few choices when/if the the time comes. Keep in mind the top of the blade will have little if any effect on your paddling. So don't stress too much on this part of the blade. As before remember what you do on the first paddle to better inform what you do on the second paddle.

Hold your blade pieces in place along side the shaft piece and test fit until you have the amount of "bend" at the top of the blade. I recommend building a bit of bend into the top of the blade.

Either way, having a mark on the shaft lets you plan on how the blade top will join the shaft, which is way better than belatedly discovering that the blade pieces are too long or short for the space you allotted at the bottom of the shaft.

Remember, once you have that first shaft piece as you want it, make a couple of marks on both the strip and the form so you can put this strip EXACTLY back in this same spot. This is important! You want to be able to easily repeat yourself. If this piece is always getting set in a different spot, your layout is always going to be different. MAKE YOUR MARKS!

Now get the second and third shaft pieces out. Loosen the compression block. Lay the second and third pieces down on top of the first piece and tighten the block a bit, but keep it loose enough that you can still slide these pieces back and forth.

To start, slide the second piece so that the bottom of this second piece is about seven inches up from the bottom of the first piece. Slide the third piece such that the bottom of it is about six inches up from the bottom of the second piece. It's kind of a "stair step" effect here. This is your first design decision. How much "offset" do you want for each piece? I recommend leaving a minimum of four inches between the bottom of the blade and the second piece. Conversely, I would go no further than about nine inches up with that second piece. Strength is mainly going to come from the epoxy and the bond it creates between the pieces, so this offset issue is about ~80% style and maybe ~20% strength.

What you are doing here is deciding how much of the first shaft piece you want exposed, how much of the second piece and the third piece? The top-most piece is going to cover the piece below it. It's a "look" that you want to affect. Some people want lots of the creamy aspen to show. Others want more of the brown cedar to show both above and/or below the aspen.
See Figure 11.

You will be removing and inserting all three of these pieces in and out of the form multiple times while you are working on the tapers, so once you decide, make some pencil marks in multiple places on both the wood strips and the form, so you can easily put the wood strips back into the same position, relative to each other and relative to the form. You want to know that the pieces are in the same position every time you move them.

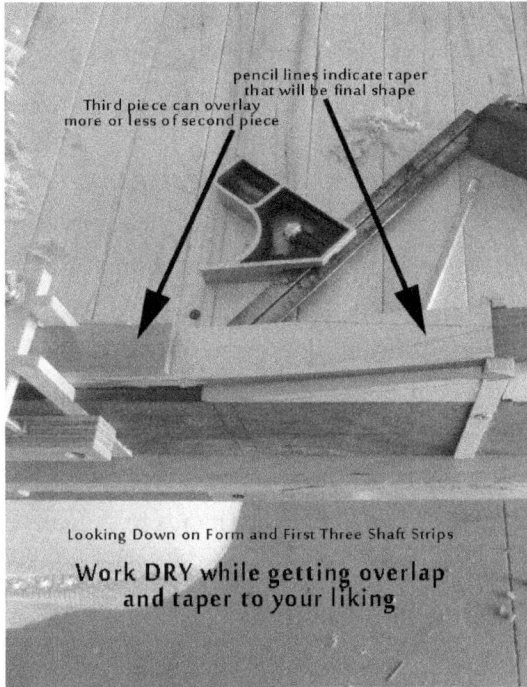

pencil lines indicate taper
that will be final shape

Third piece can overlay
more or less of second piece

Looking Down on Form and First Three Shaft Strips

Work DRY while getting overlap
and taper to your liking

Figure 11: Dry Fitting the First Three Pieces and Drawing in the Tapers

At this point you might be anxious to start joining the pieces. Stay away from the GFlex for now, we still need to taper the ends of the second and third pieces. Running through this initial shaping while dry is fairly stress free. Once you do the the GFlex there's no turning back, at least without making a sticky mess.

TAPERING THE SHAFT PIECES

First of all have a look at Figures 11 and 12, so it is clear just what a "taper" looks like. Most paddle makers don't want square ends and full thickness shaft strips stacked on top of each other, which is what you have now. Take the stack apart and lay the second and third strips down on your bench. Draw in some pencil lines to make a taper or a blunt tip. This tip shape can be of your choosing, it is not all that functional it is mostly style. A three inch taper seems to work for my eye.

Using a square of some sort makes it easy to get the start of both sides at the same point, which keeps the taper looking even. A Japanese pull saw works nicely here to cut along the lines and remove most of the wood. But just about any saw will do. Saber saws and table saws are hard to work with given narrowness of the piece and the angled cut. Hand-powered tools are much easier to work with relative to electric powered tools. With the big chunks cut off, the rough shape of the taper is apparent. Now use the spokeshave, rasp(s), sandpaper, your eye and your hands to thin down the taper at the end of the second and third pieces into the final form that you see in your head. Gradually bring each piece to a point or a snout if you want. To me, this is tapering which is what I call this process.

I like standing up and bracing the end of the form and angle block against my stomach while I hold the spokeshave with both hands and pull it towards me. I need to shove the first piece down to do this as you'll see. Place the spokeshave at your taper line and lightly pull it towards you. All you're doing here is thinning that shaft piece down to the thickness that you see in your mind's eye. It doesn't have to be super thin and pointy. Try for that first small curl of a shaving. Just get a feel for how the tool works. It might take some adjusting. Vary pressure, how much of the blade is exposed, and the angle of the tool relative to the wood. See Figure 12.

Figure 12: Second Shaft Piece with Taper Thinned and Sanded

Note this same process will happen with the fourth piece as well, but I recommend doing the first three pieces in a unit and then joining them and then moving onto the fourth and fifth pieces. The fourth piece is barely in the bend and does not usually get as much tapering as the first three. The fifth piece is not in the bend at all and both the bottom and top ends are tapered and "flowed" much more than any of the first four pieces.

Assembling the shaft can take a while. Be patient. I work on the first three pieces together as a unit. In addition to using the form, I like laying each piece flat on a work bench and shaping them. I also work each piece individually while it is clamped on the form. Sometimes I just pull the second piece over the top of the first piece while still in the form and work on it that way. This is an iterative gradual process. Be patient. You get better at this as you work your way through it. Check all three pieces together throughout so you know what you are getting. Most of the time I **take the first piece out in order to protect the edges** while I am tapering the second and third pieces.

OPTION ASIDE - Some people ask if it is easier to attach the blade pieces to the first shaft piece before the bending is done. No is the short answer. I have found that adding the blade pieces first, introduces additional stiffness to the first shaft piece in the bend area. With blade attached that first shaft piece is more bend resistant and may suddenly snap. If it breaks, now you not only have a broken shaft piece, but blade pieces are attached to the broken shaft piece. Now you have to stress out about how to cut out the broken shaft piece so you can reuse the blade pieces.

Still, it can be done this way. I DO NOT do it. I DO NOT recommend it. But if you are a rebel or don't like instruction books, give it a go and see what happens. I did kind of warn you though, and the warning is based on my own painful experience. **END ASIDE**

OPTION ASIDE If you have not used a spokeshave before, now is the time to practice on some scraps. Get a feel for your spokeshave first on some scrap. Use the vise on your workbench. If you do not have a vise and a bench, a simple clamp on the edge of a counter can work in a pinch as well. I also like using the form, both with and without the angle block as a sort of mini workbench to hold the pieces while I shape the tapers.

The spokeshave itself may require some adjusting of the edge in and out of the throat piece. Start with the sharp edge not exposed at all. Lay the spokeshave flat on a piece of scrap so you can get a feel for what the flat base feels like. That's the first thing. Then loosen the setscrew and give each thumbscrew a half turn. Pull it along the edge of your test board. Take note of the feel and the size of the emerging curl (if any). Continue a half turn at a time until the blade has emerged the tiniest bit. Feel that bite. Angle it and pull it towards you. Look at the curl that emerges out of the throat. Sometimes that throat will clog and this can cause the spokeshave to skip and chatter, so watch that throat and clear it of clogs as soon as they occur. Be patient. Don't over muscle it. Try different angles and positions. Once you have a feel for pulling the spokeshave across wood, it's time to get real.

Hit Google and especially Youtube and check out some videos on how people use the spokeshave. This book also has an accompanying DVD with plenty of footage starring a spokeshave (hint hint). It is a great tool!

I tend to pull my spokeshave towards me. I like the view better and feel it gives me the control I want. It can be pushed however. The mohunter68 video[2] below for example, is pushing it rather than pulling it, but other than that I agree with everything he says. I don't

---

2

www.youtube.com/watch?v=bClutZgLM4Y

really even disagree with his pushing the tool. I just don't use it that way.

Note that you can also find videos on sharpening a spokeshave and the other tools which will need to be done sooner or later. **END ASIDE.**
Back to the first three shaft pieces.

The bottom of the first piece, the one that the blade pieces will attach to, does not really get touched in this tapering process. I try and protect that first piece as much as I can, so it does not get any dings or nicks. Keep the edges as square and undamaged as you can. This will give you a nice tight fit with the blade pieces. You will be using that first piece though, to check how the other two shaft pieces look on top of it, so don't put it too far away.

Make sure you make plenty of marks on both sides of both the form and the wood strips, both close to the bend and way down at the handle end, so you can easily repeat your positions once you start removing and inserting the wood pieces.

Push the third piece back and have a go with the spokeshave on the second piece. Try the first pull. You may get nothing. Change your angle and try again. At this point you are getting a "feel" for the tool. After a few minutes on the second piece pull the third piece back into place and work on it a little bit. Line all three pieces up and get a feel for how the tapers all look together.

Just like anything worth doing, working a spokeshave takes a bit of practice. Be patient and change tool positions and see what each angle feels like. You get better with practice! See Figure 12, which shows the second piece with a completed taper overlaying the first piece.

As you move the pieces around on the form, you'll likely start using the compression block to hold things in place. Generally breaks start out as small snaps or crackles. It rarely just goes all at once without any warning signals. Pay attention when you are test fitting and checking your curve. If you hear a crackle (smaller sound than a snap) immediately release the tension before the break progresses any further.

OPTION ASIDE - What happens if the shaft strip breaks? See the FAQ section for notes on possibly recovering from this with a scarf joint. **END ASIDE**

Fun with Epoxy

With the tapers on the second and third pieces complete, we're getting close to show time. Cover the form itself with a long piece of wax paper. Yes common wax paper, the kind you might use to wrap your sandwiches, works quite well for preventing unwanted epoxy from bonding pieces together. In this case you do NOT want to bond the shaft strips to the underlying form.

When you tighten the wing nuts on the compression blocks, there will be some squeeze-out of the epoxy from in between the pieces. Squeeze-out is part of the process. The wax paper is the perfect low tech barrier for stopping the squeeze-out from drying and bonding the shaft piece to the underlying form. Do frequently check the wax paper and make sure there are not any rips or tears. I use a sharp edge to make small cuts in the wax paper on top of each alignment bar and then push the paper down over the bar until the wax paper is laying flat on the form. Finally, I add a second piece of wax paper in kind of a "U" shaped cradle inside each of the alignment bar pairs. See Figure 13.

Lay that first shaft piece back in its original position on the form. You can easily do this because you made all those marks remember? Make sure that second layer of cradling wax paper is nice and smooth and standing up straight. You may need to loosen the alignment blocks a tiny bit to allow for the increased thickness that the wax paper adds.

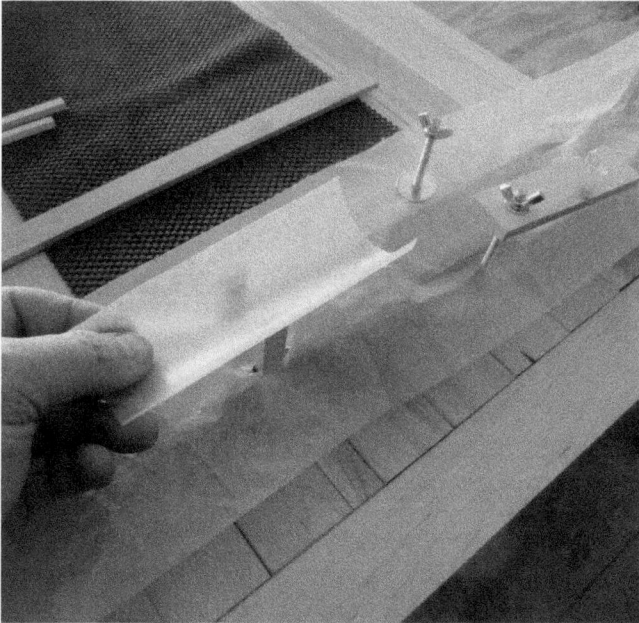

Figure 13: A wax paper cradle inside alignment bars and on top of form

Before we go any further, let's consider the handle for a paragraph or two. First of all, the sky is the limit here. I find the handle to be the most complex piece of the whole project. If you have ideas, feel free to pursue them. Again, no rules preventing you from making the handle that you want to make. Before you run off though, go look at Figure 14. This shows how a one piece quietwater handle and the shaft pieces connect. Note in Figure 14 that the shaft pieces fit into a mortise in the handle. This covers the end grain and creates a nice strong connected piece. Also note the top inch of that first shaft strip is notch shaped in order to fit in a notch that has been let in to the handle. This can be shaped with a saw, it can be carved or even sanded until the fit between notch end of shaft and the notch on the handle allows for that inch of fit for the shaft into the mortise.

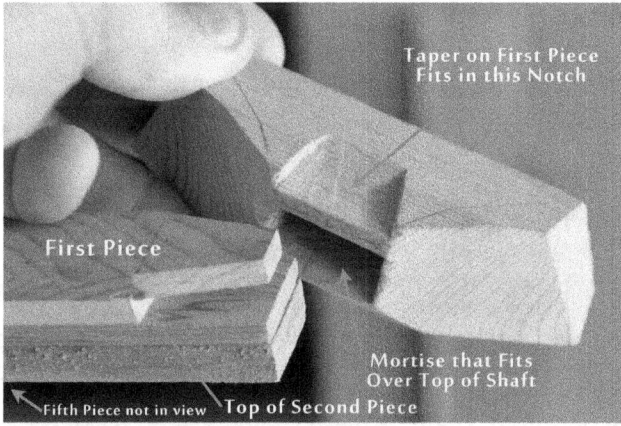

Figure 14: Closeup of the Handle and its Connection with the Shaft Pieces

Creep up on this a bit at a time. It is finesse work. If the outer edges of the notch on the handle chip, that is OK, much of this is removed during shaping and sanding anyway.

The quietwater handle has both a mortised hole for the main shaft and a notch to fit the first piece. There is a piece of wood in between the mortise and the notch. This is designed to fit crosswise in between the first and third shaft pieces. This means you need to cut the second shaft piece an inch shorter so that you have room to fit that cross piece in place. Check out Figure 14 above to see what I do with quietwater handles. This is one design piece I recommend regardless of what you may come up with on your own. The surface area allows for a strong bonding surface. It also allows for a single piece of long grain wood to resist the torque that is applied to the handle when it is in use. Gluing short pieces of wood against either side of the shaft tends to be a weaker connection. The one piece going through, gives that strength, and resistance to twisting, especially when all the other pieces are epoxied to it. That said, I have found a one piece handle to be better overall.

You can work from scratch at this point and devise your own original work. Feel free to look at my handle and try to copy it. It'll take some time and likely several iterations. Or you can develop something different. Some of my early versions were simply short pieces of strip wood glued together and then cut into shape with a band saw. Lots of possibilities here. Enjoy this process. I think the handle is far and away the most complex piece of this project.

Back to the shaft. At this point you should know how tall/long you want to make your paddle. Get that first shaft piece in place on the form. The bottom of the first piece should extend beyond the end of the angle block. To measure length I put the form at a right angle to a wall and gently butt the bottom of the first shaft piece as it sits in position on the angle block against the wall. With a tape measure I now simply measure the distance from the wall out to the end of the shaft.

Now lay the second piece in on top of the first. Make sure your marks line up. Now make a mark on that second piece an inch down from the top end of the first piece. This gives you space for the cross piece of the handle. Hopefully Figure 14 makes this clear. It's harder to write about it than it is to just show it! Take the second piece off the form and cut it to length.

At this point, I usually lay down a continuous sheet of six-inch wide wax paper on the top of the form, including the angle block.

Simple wax paper does a great job of preventing epoxy from bonding the shaft to the form. USE IT! You won't regret this step.

You are still working **DRY** at this point. Lay the fist piece back in place and align with marks. Lay that cut-to-length second piece down on top of the first piece one last time. Make light marks on the first piece where the tapered part of the second piece taper will be positioned. I don't smear any epoxy in this area on the first piece. For this tapered space, I apply the epoxy to the underside of the tapered area on the second piece. It makes a bit less of mess and puts the epoxy right where the bond needs to happen. Excess epoxy that dries on the first piece is hard to sand and finish.

Check your pieces one last time. **NOW** mix up your first batch of GFlex epoxy. You're doing one join at a time so you don't need a gallon of it. Just a tablespoon or so. Save some coffee cups and reuse them as mixing cups or go find some small cups. Lots of options. However big you make the batch, with Gflex it is equal parts resin and hardener. Small quantities. Start with a tablespoon or so. Squirt the resin and hardener directly into the mixing cup. I like to hold the mixing cup at an angle and squirt the hardener directly from the bottle into the cup until I think the puddle is approximately one tablespoon in size. See Figure 15.

Figure 15: GFlex Hardener and Mixing Cup

Then squirt an equal amount of the resin into the cup right on top of the hardener. I like small batches. I think it is better to run out of an epoxy batch and make an even smaller next batch than it is to have a large quantity left over that goes to waste. That is an expensive piece of garbage. Remember if you use GFlex epoxy it is mixed in a 1:1 ratio. Equal parts of both. I think it is easier to eyeball small quantities and judge them equal as you are squirting each liquid into the mixing cup. Larger quantities are harder to judge. Another reason to mix small batches. GFlex is fairly forgiving in my experience, so the quantities do not need to be equal down to the nano-unit. Just do your best to make the quantities equal.

It's time. Finally. With that first shaft piece in place, the wax paper in place and the second piece now removed (again) I use a wood scrap about a half-inch wide and scoop out a bit of the epoxy from the cup and smear it onto the top surface of that first piece. I scoop and smear and rub up and down the length of the first piece. The goal is a thin uniform layer of epoxy. Not too thick. I try and scoop up any runs I see that spill over the side. It is usually a bit messy. Hold the wax paper cradles up straight as you smear the epoxy in the area between the alignment bars.

There's compromise here in applying the epoxy. Too much epoxy is only going to get squeezed out and wasted, too little and you'll compromise the integrity of the bond. Also, I find that with too much epoxy the strips don't make contact and tend to slide around and not want to stay where I put them. I go for a nice "film" of epoxy. It's hard to estimate, but I would write that the film is less than 1 millimeter thick. I don't measure it. What I notice more than anything is that the wood changes color as the epoxy covers it.

Just smear some on and go for it. This is one of those simple things that take more words to describe it than it should. Just do it.

I cover the first piece up to the point where the tapered portion of the second piece begins. I then smear some on the **UNDERSIDE** of that second piece **JUST ON** the tapered section. If you do this, make sure you smear on the correct side!

Now carefully lay the second piece down in the form on top of the first piece. Check your marks as you lay it in place. The alignment bars do most of the work. Gently pull up on the wax paper cradles, as you push the second down onto the first piece. Make sure the wax paper does not get sandwiched in between the shaft pieces. Start pushing the second piece down with your fingertips, checking the marks while doing so. **MAKE SURE** the taper is right side up. Now put the compression blocks across the top of the second piece and push them down until contact is made. Start tightening the wing nuts equally on both sides. Go up and down the form pushing the pieces together and tightening the wing nuts. Make sure everything is aligned.

I start with the clamp nearest the bend, so I can keep an eye on my marks and make sure the pieces stay where I want them as the pressure is applied. At the clamp nearest the bend, tighten the wing nuts down enough to get the bend into shape. Make sure the large fender washer is on TOP of the block. This helps distribute the pressure across the block. Now tighten the other two compression blocks down most of the way **BUT NOT TOO TIGHT**. Go back to the first block and tighten a bit more. Get your eye involved and sight down the shaft as best you can, checking for straightness. Back to the second and third blocks. Tighten them some more. Observe the joint. When it looks tight and epoxy starts to ooze out from between the pieces you have probably tightened things enough.

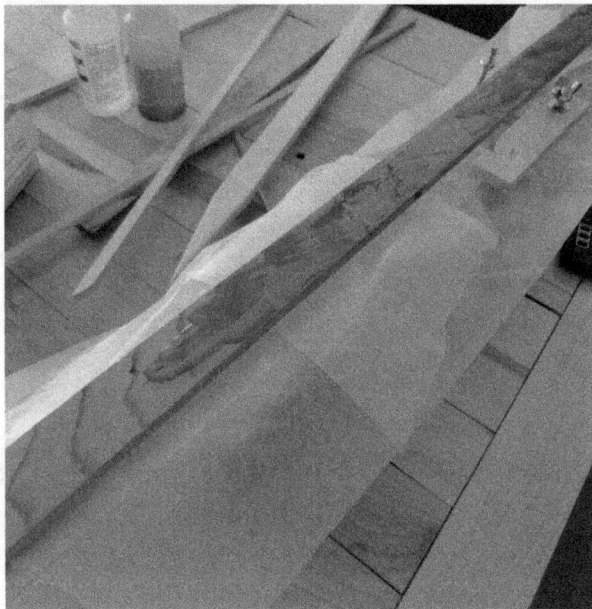

Figure 16: Thin Layer of GFlex Spread Over Top of First Piece

Go back and check out the bend. Make sure the point of the taper is centered and that things look symmetrical. Now is the time to loosen the clamp and adjust the wood if needed before the epoxy starts to set. Resist the urge to crush it a little more to get rid of the gap below the apex of the curve. Leave the gap alone. It's fine.

Now go away for several hours. Let this joint rest, cure, dry, and get strong. West Systems, the maker of GFlex recommends three hours at a minimum. I usually do overnight. But doing one lamination first thing in the morning (assuming it is warmer than 60 degrees) and a second later in the day can be OK too. Air temperature, humidity, and how much hardener is in the epoxy all combine to control the drying rate.

The next morning or later in the day you will arrive at **THE MOMENT OF TRUTH**. It is time to remove the clamps and take this paddle shaft out and see how it looks. Cautiously release the wing nuts. I evenly release the pressure from both sides. There might be a few pops as the pressure is released. The shaft might stick to the wax paper a little bit. Lift it up out of the form. If the wax paper is sticking, just slowly peel it off. If the shaft is stuck to the form, look closely at where it is stuck. A razor blade, Xacto knife or some delicate chisel work is usually enough to separate the form from the shaft.

You should now have a two-piece bent shaft that you can pick up and hold in your hand. Hold it gently. No waving around quite yet, it's still curing. I am always surprised how much stiffer and stronger two epoxied pieces are when together and dry relative to two individual pieces.

Celebrate wildly. Keep the latent engineer bottled up. You're more of a primitive person now, celebrating the simple things.

It will be a little ugly. No matter how much you minimize the squeeze out you will not eliminate squeeze out. There may even be dried epoxy UNDER the first piece. No worries at this point. I usually do the third piece before I use the block plane and cabinet scraper to remove the squeeze out from the shaft stack.

OPTION ASIDE While I dislike talking about the negative, if something went wrong, at this point the two pieces may have popped apart, leaving you back at square one. Look at both pieces, the epoxy, etc. Figure out where it went south. Make sure you are using the GFlex epoxy and mixing it as close to a 1:1 ratio as you can. It's not exact. It is somewhat forgiving. This is a chemical process, that relies on the presence of the hardener to "force" the resin to cure. This is a good opportunity to learn about using scrapers. This tool does a great job removing dried epoxy. So you may be able to reuse these popped apart pieces. If not, grab a couple new pieces. Save the old pieces, maybe they will work for one of the shorter pieces.**END ASIDE**

Time for the third piece - If you have not already done so now, before you join the third shaft piece, is the easiest time to cut the second shaft piece to the right length so as to make the notch for that handle piece to fit.

What are you going to know later that you don't already know now? This really is the best time to decide on a finished height. Do that and then cut this second piece to the right length.

Put the two-piece bent shaft back in the form. Align it with those marks on the form you made earlier. Check your wax paper. The third strip has already been tapered. So mix up another small batch of GFlex and smear it on top of the second piece. Same process as the first time. I avoid epoxy in the taper area, preferring instead to smear the epoxy on the bottom of the third piece in lieu of the second piece top. Easier cleanup and less wasted epoxy.

Lay that third strip in place. Remember, this piece is another six (or whatever you chose) inches further up the shaft. Check your marks. Only a little of this strip should be part of the bend. Up at the handle end remember to make sure this third piece is the same length as the first piece. NOT shorter like the second shaft piece is. Check it over, as before, tighten the wingnuts and let it dry.

When the third piece is done, you can clean up the squeeze out a bit if you want, or go right back and repeat one more time with the fourth piece (cedar again). It's kind of up to you and your designer eye to determine how much (if any) of this fourth piece is part of the bend. I recommend at most only a few inches should be in the bend. With this piece the rectangle from which you will shape the oval or egg-shaped shaft piece begins to appear. Do your now familiar epoxy joining. Let it dry and come back for...

One more piece. The fifth and final shaft piece. Shortest one of all. No bend. This piece will taper out before it gets to the throat area and the bend area. I usually make this a piece of poplar.

With the fifth piece dry, you are done with the assembly of the shaft. On to shaping and sanding the shaft, adding the blade and the doing the handle. More wild celebration is appropriate here if you have any left in the tank.

Read the section on Shaft Shaping and Sanding **BEFORE** you attach the blade pieces. I like to do most of the shaft shaping **BEFORE** I add the blade or the handle. You may also want to do most of the blade shaping prior to joining the blade pieces with the shaft.

In this book, I put the assembly process as its own section and the shaping process as its own section. In project work, you will most likely be going back and forth between assembly and shaping. This is OK, first time paddle making may not be the most linear project you have ever done.

[4]

Paddle Making - the Blade

Just as a matter of reference, there are six blade pieces in the quietwater kit, two big half teardrop shaped cedar pieces, two narrow aspen pieces, and two edge trim purpleheart pieces. Given the freedom you have, you can rip your own pieces and mimic the quietwater style or you can laminate several strips together to create the familiar breadboard pattern blade blank. From that blank you can then cut your rough shapes and attach to the shaft piece as you see fit. Or, you could buy blade pieces from quietwater (one more hint sorry).

These pieces are all fairly flexible at this stage. Keep in mind that the stiffness of the paddle blade comes from the epoxy and fiberglass. I see the wood as giving shape and color. The epoxy and fiberglass give the strength and stiffness.

As you cut your pieces, be sure and protect the edges as much as you can. Knicks and dings in the edges create noticeable little shadows when you start joining the pieces together. Yes, this is from painful experience. Cedar in particular, is a very soft wood. It is surprising how easy it is to put a gouge or scratch into the blades, especially the edges. I try hard to keep those inner edges at full thickness and with sharp corners so that they will join up tightly with the shaft or narrow pieces, depending on what you are using. You might put tape on this edge to remind you not to touch it. See Figure 17.

Make small pencil marks across both pieces and the shaft once you have everything aligned the way you want. The pencil marks make it easier to lay things back out in the same position facing the same direction, if you are taking down and moving around.

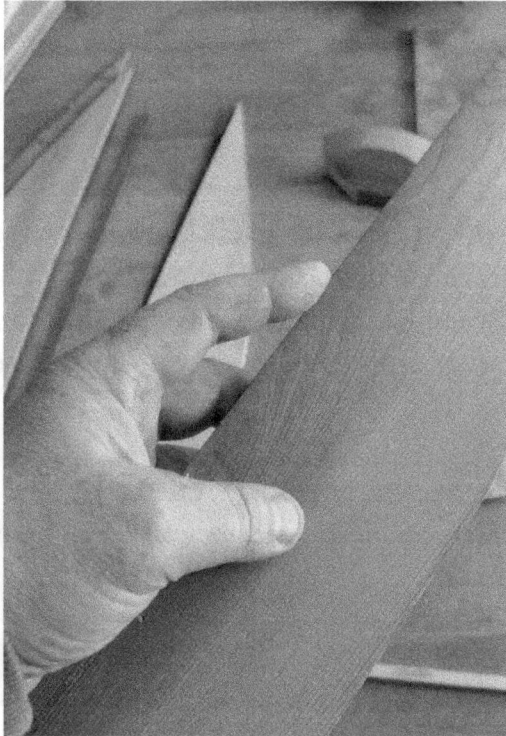

Figure 17: Protect the inner edge of the big blade pieces

The first exercise is to work a taper into the big half blade pieces from their full thickness inner edge to the outer edge. This is done to BOTH sides of the piece. A simple block plane works well for this. It can be an aggressive tool, so go just one or two strokes at a time. Cabinet scrapers and spokeshaves also work well for this.

Figure 18: Scraper in Action, Notice Angle and Fingers

There are several options to hold the blade piece while you work it. Dogs and a workbench are nice. A piece of scrap lumber and a clamp used to press the piece down onto the counter top can get the job done. A clamp with a rubber pad can work. I have a piece of 2x6 with numerous holes drilled in it that fit the dogs. I clamp the 2x6 to the counter and use the dogs in the holes. I can flip the piece over to the other side of the board and also easily move the dogs to fit the new position of the blade piece. Work on the edge of your table so that your outside hand can drop below the surface of the work area. This makes it MUCH easier to work at an angle to make the taper. Vary the pressure, angle, and bend you put into the scraper. The DVD that goes with this book shows scrapers in action (hint hint). YouTube also has examples of scrapers doing their thing. They are a great simple tool.

I generally use the plane and the scrapers. The plane removes the big volume of wood. The scrapers make the damage from the plane look nice. The sandpaper makes everything better, especially if you start with the 120 and work slowly through all the grits.

Be patient. Keep at it. Flip the piece often. Work both sides. Work both pieces. Use all three scrapers. Use different edges of the scrapers.

I go to sandpaper when the final shape is close. The cedar blades are very soft and their broad surfaces will reveal scratches quite easily under the final coat, so only use the 100 grit if something is seriously wrong, otherwise start with 120 and move to the 150 grit as soon as you can.

It's been my experience that you need only a bit of taper from the inner edge of the blade to the outer edge of the blade. Start out thinking $1/32^{nd}$ off of each side to make the taper. Starting with a ¼-inch ($8/32^{nds}$) piece, removing $2/32^{nds}$ is already removing 25% of the edge thickness. This is easy to overdo, especially with the block plane.

Remember there are two sides to the blade. It's possible that you might want one side of the blade pieces to face forward or backward. If you have a preference, mark the blade lightly with a pencil so you can see which side goes which way. Again, **REMEMBER** to taper the blade pieces on both sides. Symmetry and balance are good things.

It can be helpful to lightly scribble with a pencil over the area you want to thin and taper. Once the pencil marks are gone you know you have evenly worked the area.

If you want to add a piece of purpleheart trim to the outer edge of the blade, keep that outer edge as square as you can. This will maximize the surface area for that small outer most trim piece to bond with. If you are not using an outer trim piece, then carefully work this outer edge to your taste.

THIN BLADE PIECES

If you are using the thin pieces, then once you have shaped the upper end (see Figures 33 and 34 up ahead), the second exercise is joining those thin pieces to the shaft. The main part of these thin pieces should not be tapered. The top two or so inches may need some thinning to match the thickness of the big blade pieces, so check the fit at the top between the thin and main blade pieces. The main shaft piece, most of the thin blade pieces, and most of the thick edge of the big blade pieces should all be the same thickness. **Skip ahead and go read the shaping section of this book; there's a section there discussing thin blade pieces.**

Dry check the fit of the thin pieces to the edge of the shaft piece. Sometimes you will need to run the plane on this edge to remove epoxy buildup that can prevent the thin piece from laying flat and fitting tightly against the shaft piece.

Once that fit looks good, lay down wax paper to cover your work area. Prop the shaft up such that the blade portion is laying flat. You might want to tape or somehow secure it so that it does not move around.

Line up the thin pieces on both sides with the shaft piece. Make sure the cut edge at the top is facing the correct way. Mix up a small batch of the GFlex epoxy (1:1 ratio) and apply it to the correct edge of the thin pieces. Same basic amount as you applied doing the shaft pieces. I like to use a kids paint brush to apply the epoxy. The brush makes for a neater job with epoxy going where I put it rather than dribbling all over. Don't worry about how much leaks out of this vertical joint and hardens against the unseen underside. If squeeze-out occurs, this is one spot where the scrapers do an outstanding job removing the dried squeeze-out. Push both thin pieces gently onto the shaft piece. Check alignment along bottom and top. Nudge up or down as needed.

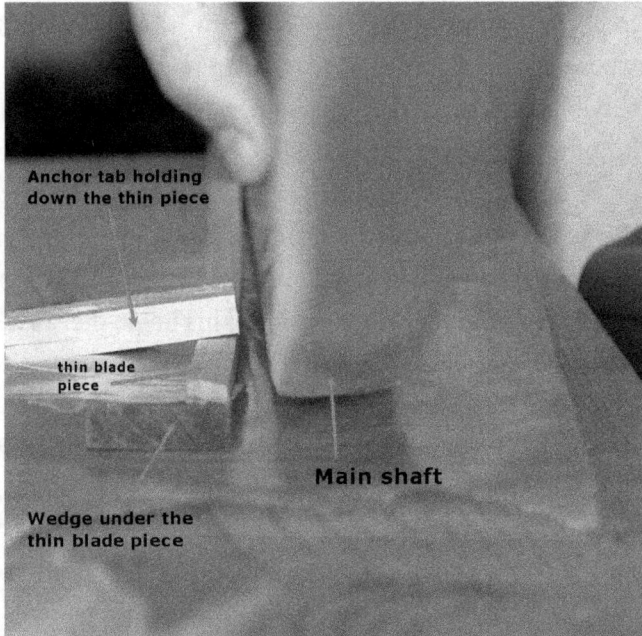

Figure 19: Making the Bend in the Blade Piece to Match the Shaft

Depending on whether you want a straight blade or a slight bend in the blade, now is when you put that slight bend into these thin blade pieces. Usually it is just in the top two inches. I use a small wedge and a scrap piece with a screw. See Figure 19 above, for a look at how I set this up to force an exact bend to match the shaft bend and then hold it there while the epoxy sets. Take a break while the epoxy on these thin pieces cures.

BIG BLADE PIECES

If you are not using the thin pieces then you will be attaching the big blade pieces directly to the main shaft. If you did use the thin pieces, now your break is over and it is time to attach the big blade pieces to the outer edge of the thin blade pieces. Sometimes a picture is worth a thousand words. See Figures 20 & 21.

Time for a **DRY TEST RUN.** Remember to put wax paper underneath the pieces before you do any epoxy work. You definitely do not want the blade pieces joined to the work surface!

I like using a couple pieces of straight-edged scrap to help with this step. A couple of short levels could also work if you have them. Clamp one piece down along the edge of your work bench. Put a big piece down against it. Now get your shaft and prop it up such that the shaft piece is level and next to the big blade piece. Phone books, scrap wood, just about anything will work to prop up the handle end of the shaft. This stack can slide up or down under the shaft to give the exact height that will get the center piece to lie flat next to the blade piece.

With the shaft laying flat next to the first big blade piece, now lay down the second blade piece on the other side of the shaft. Next to that lay the second straight piece of scrap. You have now sandwiched the blade in between the two scrap pieces. Outboard of this second scrap place something heavy like a ten pound weight plate, or a brick, or even a pot full of water. Recall the first straight piece is clamped in place, this second piece is still loose. Gently slide it in and start snugging it up against the outer edge of the second blade piece. Keep snugging it up until both blade pieces are making firm contact with the shaft.

Figure 20: Looking Down on the Wedge and Edge Setup for Joining Blade and Shaft – remember the wax paper!

Keep moving your weight in against the outer side of your straight edge as well, this serves to anchor that second straight edge in place. Before you get too excited with securing the pieces in place, have a look at the bottom end view. First of all make sure the ends of all five pieces are even. Next check that you see the big blade pieces butting squarely against the shaft piece or the thin pieces. While the inner edge is tight and square against its neighbor, the outer edge has that slight taper. Squat down at the end of your bench and look at the end view of the blades and center shaft. Make sure this is flat. You want to check that there is just a tiny bit of space underlying that outer edge.

Figure 21: a More Ornate Jig for Working the Bend into Tip of the Blade

This may be hard to see, it is only about $1/32^{nd}$ of an inch after all. I use folded up wax paper to support this outer edge while it dries. Position the folded wax paper under the outer edge of the blade to support it in a straight flat position while the epoxy dries.

Once the positioning is complete, I add a clamp and a scrap piece of wood across the bottom of the paddle to keep it all flat. I like a scrap about four inches long such that the center shaft and the thickest part of both blades are affected. I place the clamp directly over the top of the center shaft piece.

With the dry test run positioning complete on the big blade pieces, take your test run all apart. **Lay down the wax paper for real this time.** Mix up another tiny batch of the GFlex epoxy. Again, a kid's paint brush makes it easier to apply the epoxy and not make a big mess. I stand up straight and hold each blade piece vertically and dab the epoxy along the length of the join area. Remember which blade piece goes down on which side of the shaft! Apply the epoxy to the inner edges of both blade pieces. Prop up the second blade piece so the epoxy does not run. Lay that first piece down in place next to the straight edge and get the center piece back in place. Make sure the wax paper is under the join area! The little piece of folded wax paper supporting the bottom outer edge may need to be repositioned, if you are even using it. Now grab that second blade piece and lay it in place. Gently push that second straight edge back into position and press your weight against that straight edge. Again not a whole lot of pressure, the joins are very small with a small amount of epoxy on a vertical surface. Don't squeeze out the epoxy! Just make a nice gentle sandwich with your two straight edge pieces.

Check the bottom edge. Make sure everything is even and flat. Tighten the clamp and the piece of scrap back down on the bottom to ensure that the blades are as flat as you can get them. Figure 20 on page 53 shows wedge pieces and small scraps. You can use them to add a bit of pressure on the upper part of the blade.

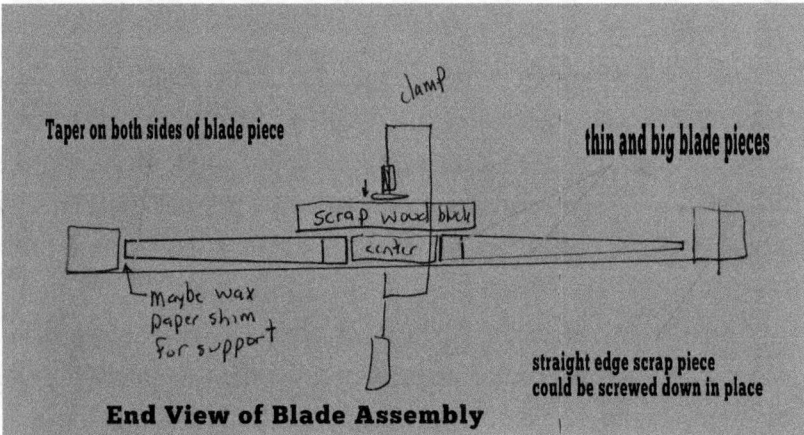

Figure 22: Drawing Showing End View of Blade Assembly

TRIM PIECES

After the big blade pieces and epoxy have dried, you can apply trim pieces along the outer edge of the blade. I like the contrast that purpleheart makes with the blade pieces. The trim pieces I use are thin. Exact thickness is not important, you need to be able to bend them along the edge of the big blade piece, that's the bottom line. Again, remember to use wax paper under the work area. Again mix up a tiny batch of GFlex. Again I like using a kid's paint brush to put the epoxy on this narrow little edge. These trim pieces need to be bent along the outer edge. The straight edge and wedge method works very well to accomplish this bend in the purpleheart, which is stiff and tends to resist bending. The purpleheart seems to accept its new shape once you have it bent and secured into position. Purpleheart also offers splinters that are unusually sharp and jagged so be careful.

A style decision comes up here involving how far you run the trim piece up the edge. You can run it all the way to the shaft if you want or end it somewhere along the edge of the cedar. I like to end it about one inch before the aspen piece with a nice tapered cut. But your mileage may vary.

With the trim pieces drying in place step back and wildly celebrate, that was the last bit of complex assembly on your paddle.

OPTION ASIDE - It's worth considering why the outer edge of the blade needs to be thinned. For me, the answer is that the outer edge of your wooden paddle blade DOES NOT need to be as thin as possible. It may be more tradition than anything. It may be more of a want than a need. I think the paddle manufacturers have marketed this "look" upon paddlers. In my opinion and experience it is not necessary to have a thin blade and/or a thin outer edge to your wood paddle blade. To be fair, with the wood sandwiched between fiberglass and epoxy, a thin edge is plenty strong, so strength or lack of it may not be much of an issue. Your mileage may vary. For me as a long time pleasure paddler, this thin edge matter is one of personal taste. This could be an opportunity to make the first paddle one way and the second paddle the opposite. You can then evaluate your results.

In my years of paddling I have never stopped in mid paddle and said, "I need a thinner edge on this blade." Blade thinness is not a parameter I have noticed much at all. I have never felt like my paddling is slower or less pleasant because of blade thickness. But this is just me. I might be a bit biased. **END ASIDE**

[5]

Paddle Making - the Handle

First of all, I try and do most of the shaft shaping prior to permanently attaching the handle. Leaving the handle off makes it easier to work the spokeshave along the length of the shaft. Figure 23

Figure 23: Handles at various stages of shaping

shows the handle style I prefer. Figure 6 back in the second chapter shows another option. You can see the two basic handle ideas, take those and either copy them or study your own ergonomics and develop a handle of your own. I do think that a piece going through the shaft in the notch created by removing the top inch of the second piece adds strength to the handle. Whatever you do, I would run a handle piece through the shaft.

Handles are a tough piece to make. The Figure 6 version of a handle contains many small pieces of wood, lots of epoxy, lots of drying time, lots of checking square and plum. The Figure 23 version combines the small pieces into one piece that is roughly cut into shape. This leaves a handle ready to attach to the shaft and ready for final shaping with hand tools.

That top final inch of the shaft, hopefully, you can leave untouched, which will ensure a tight fit into the mortised hole in the base of the handle. That does leave the other forty some odd inches to shape though!

For the one piece handle, I gently push the handle down over the top of the shaft. The mortised hole is one inch deep. The fit should be tight. Carefully trim the edges of the mortise itself or the shaft as well as the notch and slowly creep on a good tight fit. This is a good spot for an Xacto knife or another sharp edge. The handle should ultimately slide down about one inch on the shaft. Be patient!

With a square, check that the handle is perpendicular to the shaft. Now, holding the paddle vertically at arm's length, look at the shaft/handle from the side. Make sure it is level and not leaning down or up, or at least positioned in such a way that you are happy. See Figure 24.

Once you run through this routine a few times and are satisfied with the handle position, mix up a tiny batch of GFlex epoxy, about ten drops, just enough to lightly coat the flat sides that will fit up in the mortise. With a fairly tight fit, there is not much room inside the mortise for the volume of epoxy so do not over do it. Coat all four sides the bottom of the second piece and the underside of the notched piece and push everything together. Run through your checks for square and plum one more time and adjust as needed. Now lay the paddle flat, notch side up so the epoxy will stay where you put it and not heed the call of gravity and run out of the handle and down the shaft.

Let this dry for several hours.

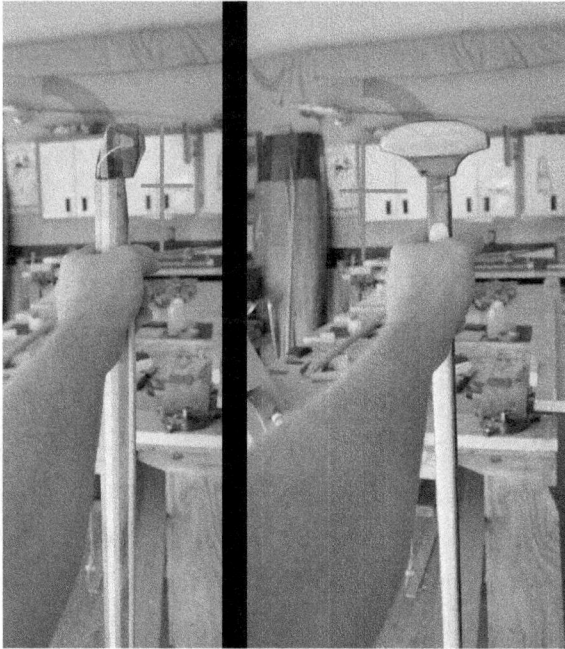

Figure 24: Hold Paddle at Arm's Length Check for Square and Plum

When this is dry, have a look at the back of the handle where the first shaft piece is fit into the notch. The notch should be fairly tight, but if there is space around the notch, you can mix up another ten drop batch of epoxy and color it with some sawdust. Take that wood-colored epoxy and carefully pack it into the notch around the tapered end of the shaft and let that dry in place. Once it is dry it can be sanded just like the wood. It's a nice decorative way to finish off the small gap around the taper. Once you have the handle joined to the shaft, you need to sand the handle into its final finished state. Parts of the handle are end grain which is a bit different from the shaft and the blade.

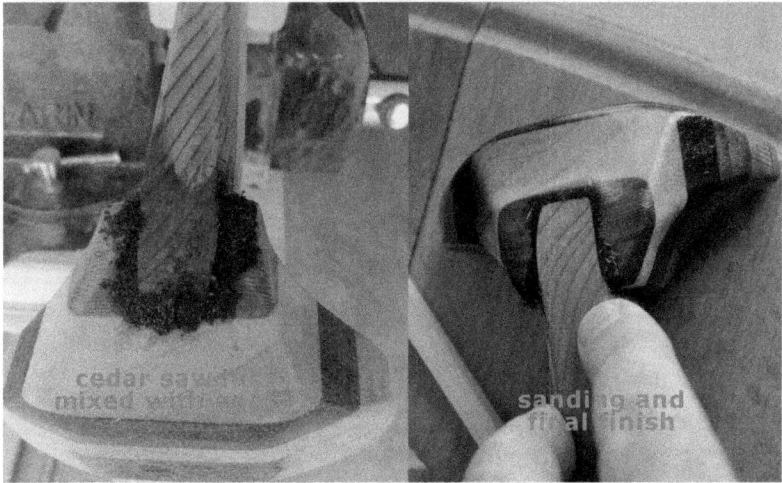

Figure 25: Handle Notch Filled with Wet Raw Epoxy and Finished Look

The same tools still get the job done. 100 and 120 grit sand paper wrapped around a variety of different round objects do most of the heavy lifting. A round Stanley surform works quite well. A plain old wood rasp can be useful. Just check your work **OFTEN**, you do not need to remove very much wood at this point. This is a gradual repetitive exercise. Hold the paddle in your hands. Switch hands. Squeeze the grip and relax. Is there an edge that you notice? Sand it down. Hold it again. Both hands. Squeeze and relax your grip. Do a j-stroke. Is that edge less noticeable? Does it need a bit more? **DO NOT** try and sand down an edge all at once. You want to "creep up" on the finished shape. Do the sand/test fit cycle three or four times, removing just a little bit every time. Work all over the handle, because as volume is removed from one part of the handle it can change how your hand fits a different part of the handle. Spend your time equally on all parts of the handle.

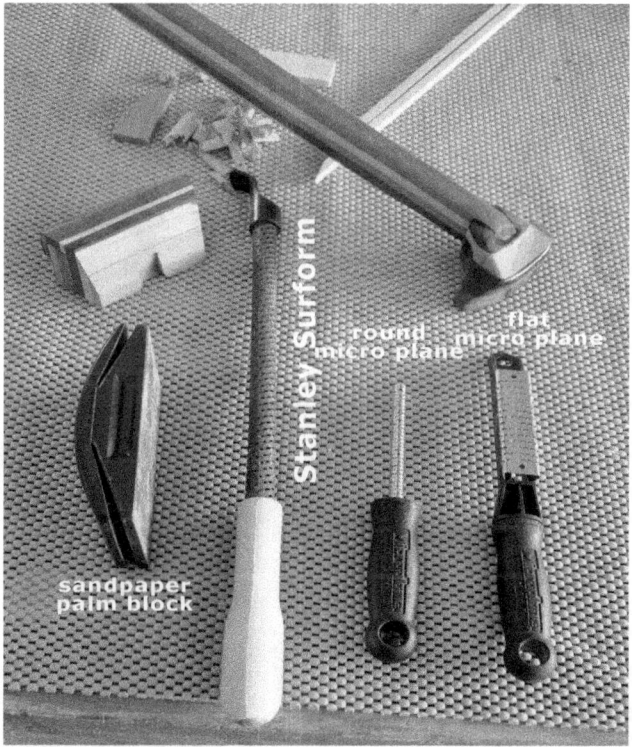

Figure 26: Some of the Shaping Tools for the Paddle Project

Three or four chunks of different size dowel or closet rod work well to wrap the sand paper around and better fit the curves of the handle. Get creative here. Wrapping sandpaper around any of several common household items can give you a profile that fits the radius of the curve you are trying to achieve.

Micro planes come in a round shape. Lee Valley (online) Wood Crafters (store and online)[3] both have a variety of shaping tools that can be useful.

Remember, it is easy to remove the wood. It is hard to add it back on. Go slow and frequently check the fit of the emerging handle with both hands. Stand on a chair so you can hold the paddle vertical.

My favorite feature of the one piece quietwater handle is that the grip is large enough to allow multiple thumb positions. You can wrap your grip all the way around the grip if you want. You can also put your thumb in more of a straight position by using the thumb pad. Moving your thumb between two positions helps prevent blisters.

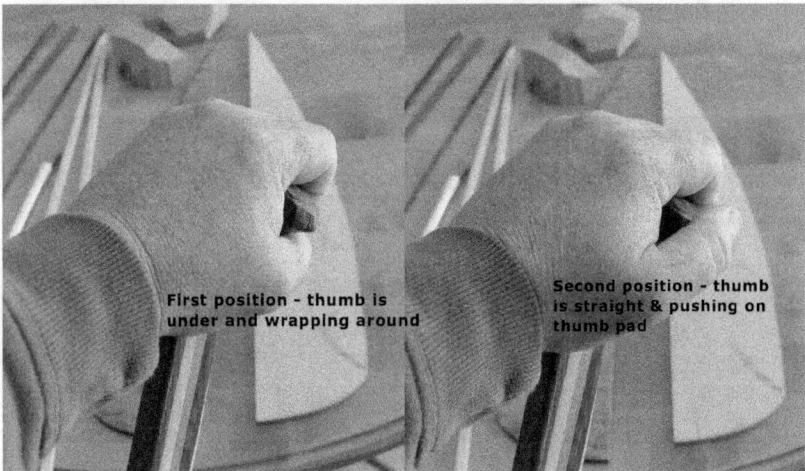

First position - thumb is under and wrapping around

Second position - thumb is straight & pushing on thumb pad

Figure 27: Two thumb positions that the handle design encourages

---

[3]Www.woodcrafters.com

[6]

Shaping and Sanding

With assembly basically done, the shaft, blade and handle all need shaping and sanding. I like doing most of the rough shaping and sanding of the shaft by itself before blade or handle are attached. Remember you can hold off on the final shaping of the shaft until after its first test paddle in real water. One part does not have to be finished before another part is started! Once the blades and handle are attached, shaping is still possible on the shaft, it's just a bit more awkward.

SHAFT SHAPING

Shaping the shaft may well be the most freeform, "artistic" part of the whole project. For starters if you have other paddles you might want to look at them and see how they taper from middle to top and middle to bottom. Many will just be round with no shaping at all. It is hard to give precise measurements for how much wood to remove. It's not very much. It is mostly according to your own feel and style. But more than anything the shape should fit your grip, both with handle and shaft. It should also of course be pleasing to your eye.

I think shaping tools are fairly simple: a spokeshave, a block plane, cabinet scrapers, and several grits of sandpaper. Lee Valley and Wood Crafters offer several tools that hold the sandpaper and make it easier to sand shapes. Dangerous in a fun way to browse these stores and websites. All sorts of useful tools. Or you can go low tech and use scrap wood or different sizes of simple wood dowels/closet rods to wrap the sand paper around. Whatever you do, keep your hands and fingers in play. They are the ultimate guides. This is not a bulk removal process, this is a small volume removal process, so don't sand for ten minutes straight. Use a tool for a few seconds at a time and check your work, before you go too far. **REMEMBER, with this soft wood, it is easy to remove and nearly impossible to put it back on!**

With all of the shaping tools, the first thing to remember is that sometimes the wood has a grain that is best worked in one direction. So be sure and move your tools in both directions on the wood surface, as one way will likely be better than the other. While I prefer pulling the spokeshave towards me and pushing the plane away from me, both plane and spokeshave can be pushed and pulled. To be clear, I also mean along the grain along the length of the shaft. I rarely ever do anything across the grain. The handle being the exception.

To my eye, the finished cross section of the shaft is kind of an egg shape with the top of the shaft being the narrow part and the bottom being the wider part. It is asymmetric, but only by a few millimeters overall.

Look at your shaft hand as it grips the shaft. The part of the shaft that will be in the crook of your fingers is the narrow part, the bottom portion of the shaft that is not contacted, is the wide part. In cross-section, I see this as a slight egg shape. A non-symmetrical oval I guess, for lack of a better phrase. If you want it to be that is. If you want a symmetrically shaped shaft that is certainly your right.

Pay attention to how much you remove from the throat area of the shaft. What is the throat you ask? The throat is what I call the top six inches or so of the shaft. Some people think this should be "slender" relative to the fat middle part of the shaft. Other people not so much. As you go about tapering from middle to top though, do recognize that this area requires patience. There are not any straight edges so plan on using good old fingers and hands to guide the sandpaper along these profiled shapes. As always, work a few minutes, stop and hold the shaft. Get a feel for it. You can always remove more. It is quite difficult to add wood back on if you go too far.

The top piece is the shortest, the least (if at all) bent and the most heavily shaped. You might consider doing some of the shaping on this piece before you epoxy it onto the fourth piece.

REMEMBER, the wood is fairly soft. The rasp and even coarse sandpaper can remove wood surprisingly fast. It's hard to put it back on. **Enjoy the process no hurrying required!**

CREATING THE FINISHED SHAFT SHAPE

Get the rough complete shaft stack secured in your vise. Using block plane and cabinet scraper, first go up and down the length of the shaft on all four of what are now flat (or at least as flat as they are going to be) sides and remove any remaining squeeze-out. You will need to move the shaft several times in the vise in order to touch all parts of the shaft. Try not to go beyond squeeze out removal on the top inch of the shaft. You want this to fit into the handle mortise as tightly as possible with square edges not rounded.

Once you've tamed the squeeze-out, go ahead and start creating the rounded profile. Both spokeshave and block plane work well to round off edges. Move the tools in both directions using light pressure.

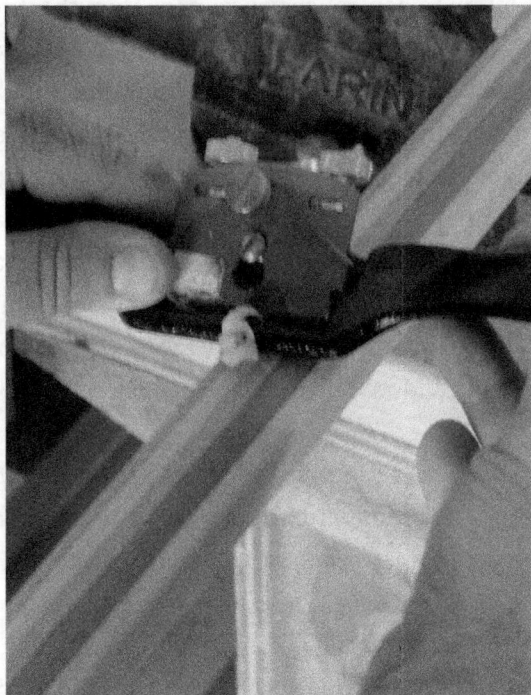

Figure 28: Spokeshave Rounding and Shaping Shaft

Overall, both spokeshave and block plane have their place in shaping the shaft. Scrapers don't work quite so well on rounding corners, but they do work well on flat surfaces. Save the 100 grit sandpaper for later. As you get further into this, there will be fewer and fewer flat surfaces, so less and less of the blade will actually be touching the wood. More of the wood will be rounded. This is what you are trying to do after all! Your shavings will get smaller and shorter as this occurs. Be patient! As you reach the end there will be no flat surfaces. Use your eye and your hands to gauge how this compound surface feels and flows around edges and along the length. Near impossible to measure with a tool, but easy to feel with your hands and see with your eye.

All you're doing is rounding off edges at this point, mostly with the spokeshave. You might try adjusting the blade in a bit, which will lessen the amount of wood that can be removed. Maybe a half turn of the adjustment screws at a time. Turn the tool over and watch the cutting edge move up into the base as you adjust the screws. Try a pull with this new edge exposed. Feel the difference in your fingers. There will be less resistance. Look at the size of the shaving that comes out of the throat. See Figure 28.

Adjust the shaft in your vise as needed and pare the wood away with the spokeshave. This is pleasantly repetitive. Work your way up or down the length of the shaft. Not all the pieces are treated the same. In Figure 29 note that the fourth and fifth pieces have more of a snout shape than a narrowly pointed taper, like pieces two and three have. The whole shaft gradually comes into shape. Try not to do too much work in any one spot. I find it easier to frequently move and touch all parts of the shaft several times each rather than trying to do one area completely before I move to the next area.

After some plane and spokeshave time, try the rasp if you have one. See Figure 31. This is a two hand tool. Use the pad of the front hand to press down on the front of the rasp. Use your back hand to push the rasp. The motion with a rasp is one of lightly sliding it obliquely across the length of the shaft while also moving it forward along the shaft. Do not go directly across the shaft. Do not apply heavy pressure on the rasp. It will QUICKLY make its mark. Always start out very gently, until you have a feel for the tool. Increase the pressure a little bit at a time.

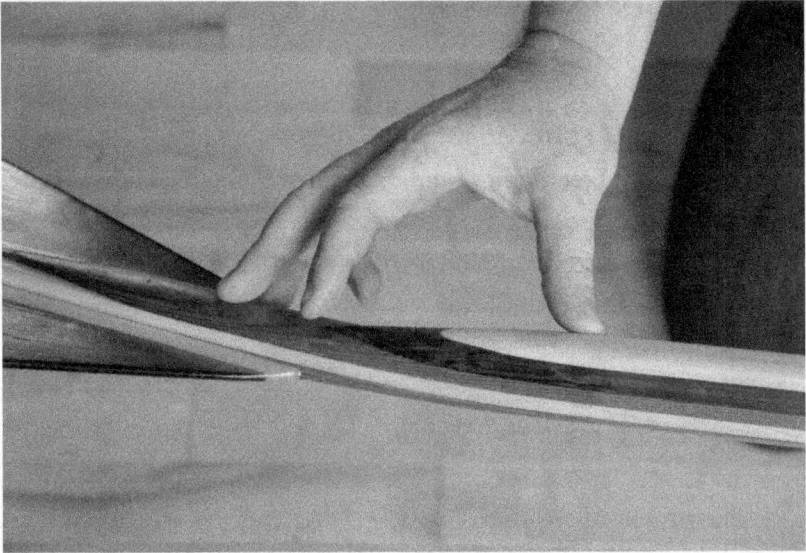

Figure 29: Lots of Options for Tapering and Finishing the Fourth and Fifth Pieces

Pushing the rasp at a 90 degree angle to the grain cuts too much and does too much "blunt force damage". A Stanley surform with a round profile is a very good variant of a flat rasp. See the yellow handle back in Figure 26.

After the rasp comes sandpaper, both in hand and in a holder of some sort. Again, holding it lightly lets the sharp edges of the sand grains do their work. Too much pressure slows things down and dampens the effect of the sandpaper. Less is more. This is somewhat counter-intuitive. Start very gently and observe the effect. Vary the pressure once you have a feel for what the paper is doing. If you have a brush you might try cleaning the surface of the paper. This can have a surprising effect. Start coarse and work your way up. Most wood, once you have ripped it into strips is going to be fairly clean and smooth. Usually, there will be no need for mass removal with coarse grits. Try 100 grit, but even that may be overkill. 120 grit is a good start followed by 150, then 180, then 220(finest).

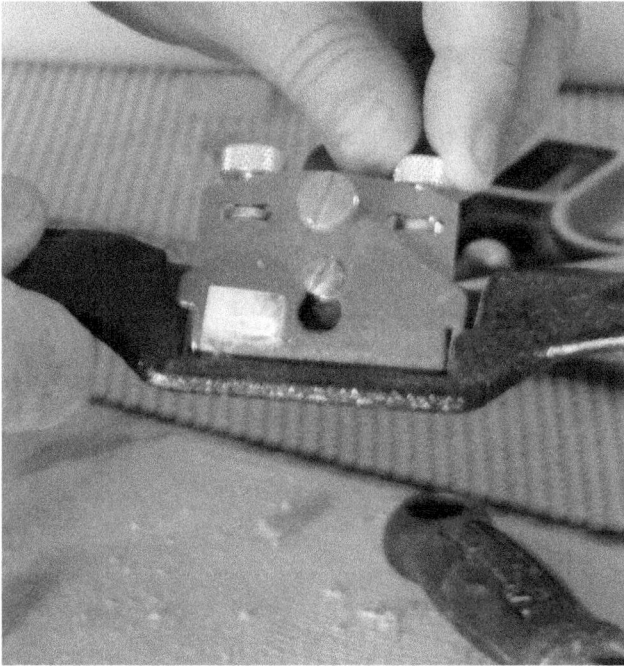

Figure 30: Adjusting blade depth set screws on a Spokeshave

Jump up in size one increment at a time. Going from 100 to 220 won't look like it is doing anything because the scratches from the 100 grit are simply too big for the very fine grains of the 220 grit to remove. The progression is important with sandpaper, skipping a grit leads to poor results.

Incidentally, hand sanding is the most strenuous part of paddle making. If you happen to sweat a lot and/or it is hot, try not to drip sweat on the raw wood surfaces. Somewhat surprisingly, I have found sweat to be a hard stain to remove from raw wood.

Achieving a final finished surface, is very much an iterative process. You need to be in a mindset that allows you to incrementally creep up on this final surface. This is a gradual process.

Experience has taught me that things happen I do not like when I am at the end of my attention span. I get anxious to finish, or I start to hurry. Or I use too much muscle and then BOOM, I have gone too far and removed too much wood, which is exceedingly hard to put back on, as I have no doubt excessively stated.

When you start to feel hurried, put your tools down and take a powder! Come back when you are relaxed.

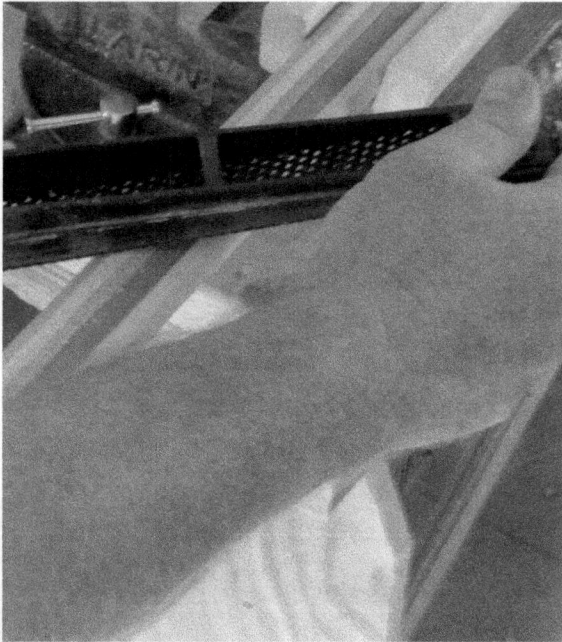

Figure 31: Using a Rasp to Shape the Shaft GO EASY with this tool!

OPTION ASIDE -An alternative to shaping at this point in the project is to go ahead and skip the shaft shaping now. Finish the blade and fiberglass it. Once that is done, go use your paddle and evaluate any further shaft shaping in the context of how it feels when you are actually using it. It may be perfectly usable as it is. The fiberglass covered blade will be good to go in the water but you might want to avoid heavy duty usage that gets that unfinished shaft all wet and water stained. Decide on any further shaft shaping, do it and then apply the final varnish to the shaft. **END ASIDE**

HANDLE SHAPING

Regardless of which basic style you choose, I think the handle is the most intricate part of this whole project. Assembly and shaping are hard to separate. The first step, earlier in the book, is trimming the notch on the first piece of the shaft to fit into the notch cutout on the handle and getting the mortise and shaft to accept each other. The shaping portion is more about where your fingertips make contact, how the leading edge of the handle feels in the crook of your fingers, and how the notch area feels in the palm of your hand

Some people like a half moon shaped curve for a leading edge, others prefer a straight leading edge. Some people like the feel of a big handful of grip, others like the feel of their hand more fully encircling the handle. Imagine that as gripping a one-inch diameter pipe versus a three-inch diameter pipe. Here again is where that test paddling can help out. Start with a big grip and a straight leading edge, use it in real water with a real canoe. With that as a guide bring it back and remove some bulk and modify that straight edge as needed.

To be clear, you're still working **DRY!** Once you have the handle fitting all the way down onto the handle, jump ahead to fiberglassing the blade. Get that done and take your paddle out for its first dip in the local water. This is not an all out effort, this first dip is to test the length of the paddle/shaft as well as testing the grip and how it feels in your hands in live conditions. The handle is designed to allow for your thumb to fit under and come to a closed grip nearly all the way around the handle. You can also move your thumb up onto the thumb pad for a change of position. Test both positions and see how they both feel.

With that initial water test done, you can take the handle off and cut the shaft to a shorter length if needed. With the length now final, you can continue working the handle while it is loose or you can now mix up a tiny batch of GFlex, coat the top inch of the shaft and/or the mortise and permanently attach the handle to the shaft. I find most of the final handle shaping is best done with the handle attached to the shaft. It is hard to shape the handle while holding it in one hand and working it with the other. It is easier to have the handle on the shaft and use both hands to hold the tools, with the shaft in the vise and the handle on the shaft.

The part of handle making I've come to like the most is that I have the option to make the handle big enough so that I can have my thumb pad out on the edge. I can also wrap my thumb under.

BLADE SHAPING

Blade shaping is fairly straightforward. I break this into two parts. The first part is working the thin blade pieces into their finished shape. Since they are attached to the shaft first (if you are using them) obviously they go first. Also these pieces are small and close to the shaft so they are hard to work once you have them joined to the shaft.

The top end should have the same angle that the big blade pieces do. Also this same top few inches of the thin pieces should be thinned to match the profile and thickness of the top of the big blade pieces. Yet one more instance where seeing it is easier than trying to describe it. Just hold the thin piece next to the big piece and make sure both match up nicely at the top end. See Figures 32 and 33.

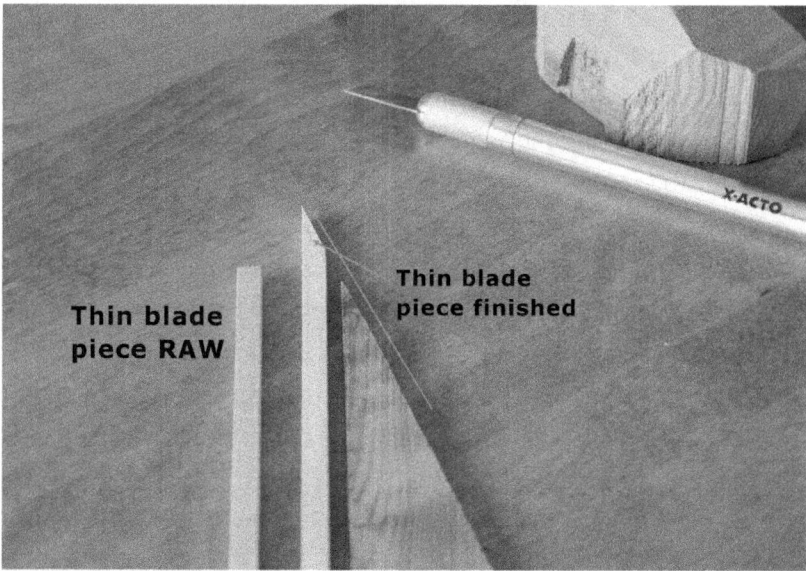

Thin blade piece RAW

Thin blade piece finished

Figure 32: Working the Thin Blade Piece to Fit the Angle Cut on the Big Blade Piece

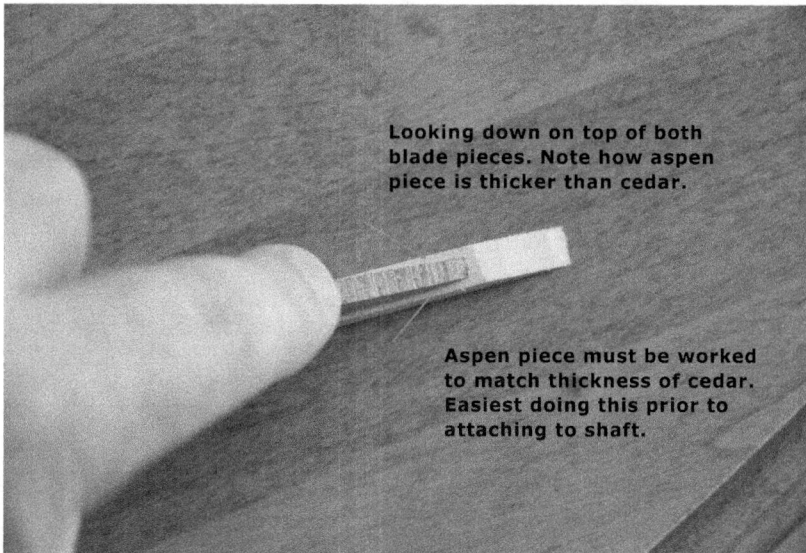

Looking down on top of both blade pieces. Note how aspen piece is thicker than cedar.

Aspen piece must be worked to match thickness of cedar. Easiest doing this prior to attaching to shaft.

Figure 33: Looking Down on Blade Pieces to Assess Differing Thickness at Top End of Blade

The second part of blade shaping is the big pieces. They have a taper, going from their thickest along the inner edge, to their thinnest along the outer edge. This taper should be applied on both sides. The taper is very slight, maybe a 1/32 off of the outer edge of the power face and another 1/32 off the back face. That makes 1/16 total, but considering that the blade starts out as 4/16ths, you are removing a significant amount of wood. As always proceed leisurely. Enjoy the process.

You will find that the blade also thins towards the top. This is OK. At least in my experience, this has been OK. This part of the blade is not a huge part of your ability to generate power. Most of the time it may not even get wet. Do check that the thin pieces and the big pieces match up at the top.

I use a block plane for this thinning and tapering process and simply clamp the blade blank on a flat surface with a scrap piece of wood on top of the blade, so the clamp does not mar the blade surface.

Bottom Profile

With the epoxy dry on the trim pieces, it is the time to consider the bottom profile of the blade. You can revisit this bottom shape after you have added fiberglass to both sides. This considerably strengthens both sides and reduces the chipping tendency of the wood. But now is a good time to at least consider the look of the bottom profile. I like a plain flattish bottom with nicely rounded corners. This is end grain, so go easy on this shaping exercise as the edges are weak. This end grain chips easily, so I avoid any big strong movements as these tend to inspire chips. Go carefully with a saw if you choose to use one. Rasps tend to break chunks of wood off this bottom edge. A Japanese pull saw can come in handy here, especially if you need to trim the purpleheart. I like 100 grit sandpaper on a five inch piece of scrap. Use double sided tape to hold the paper on the wood. This is easy to hold and rotate as you work this edge into shape.

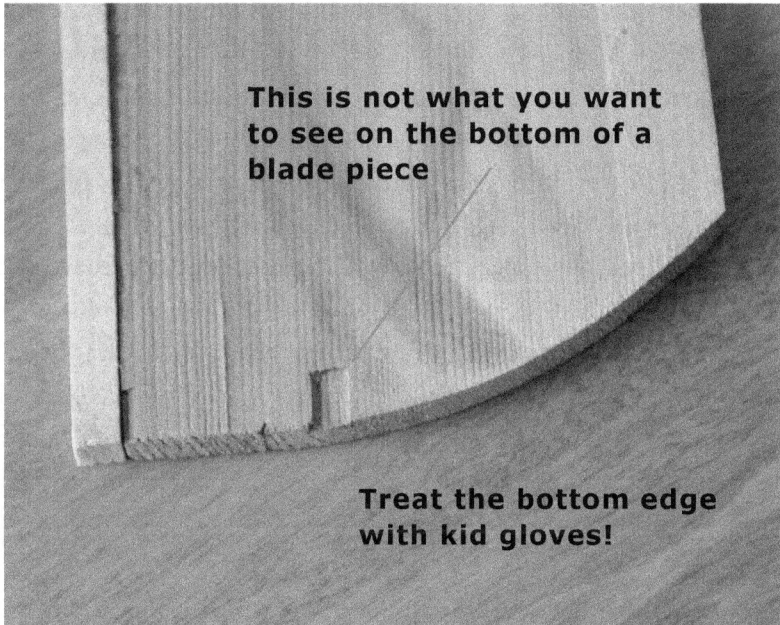

Figure 34: Rough Handling of the Bottom Edge Leads to Chips

Again, you can also revisit this bottom shape after you have added fiberglass to both sides. This considerably strengthens both sides and reduces the chipping tendency of the wood.

FINAL FINISH SANDING

Here is where the final appearance really comes into view. Here again patience is required. Let the sandpaper do its work with a minimum of downward pressure, or at least an awareness of how much pressure you are exerting relative to the wood removal you are creating. At this point less can be more.

One benefit of hand sanding is the dust tends not to get kicked up in the air as much as power tools tend to do. You will also generate a far smaller volume of sawdust. The dust you do generate tends to be visible to the human eye. Regardless of whether you use hand or power tools for sanding, it's probably not the best idea to breathe in sawdust. Dust masks are widely available (same section as ear plugs in the hardware store). You can also keep your work area well ventilated, in fact working outdoors could well remove the sawdust from your breathing space quite well. Take frequent breaks. Blow your nose and check the tissue to see just how much dust you are expelling. If you can feel it in your throat or chest, if you find yourself coughing, or your eyes are irritated as you work, you are probably creating and breathing too much airborne dust. You need to remove the airborne irritant. Change your work conditions and/or add protective gear as needed.

If you choose to use some funky exotic wood (e.g. of African or South American origin), some of those woods can be poisonous if breathed. Be sure and ask the store where you bought the wood if there are any issues with sanding and breathing any dust you might create from this foreign exotic wood.

In no particular order, here are some things that run through my mind as I am sanding:

- circular movements can leave circular marks on the wood surface, especially if there is a strong grain pattern present. Use this motion just be sure and go over it with a progression of finer grit papers, brush or wipe the surface clean and use reflected light or a direct light source to get a clear view of what that surface looks like.

- It's worth repeating - light is your friend, look at your piece from all sides, look at it standing straight up, look at it bent over with your eye at the same height as the paddle surface. Move around check check check for swirl or other line marks. On the blade surfaces, these marks, if they are big enough, can show through the fiberglass and epoxy.

- When sanding the shaft, I often put the sandpaper across the palm of my hand and then lightly grip the shaft and move up and down.

- In general I do not sand across the grain ever.

- That being said, the handle sometimes requires sanding across the grain.

- The bottom of the blade may need some sanding. This is all end grain with the sanding motion going across the grain. I hold off sanding or shaping this bottom edge until I have the fiberglass on both sides of the blade. This strengthens the wood and lessens the odds of chipping off a piece of the blade surface due to an awkward sanding motion. See Figure 34 for a painful result of working the bottom edge a bit too vigorously while it was unstrengthened by fiberglass and epoxy.

- When sanding along the edge where the soft cedar is joined with the harder aspen, you may remove more of the cedar than you do of the aspen, simply because the aspen is harder and more resistant to sanding. So be careful along edges where one wood is much harder or softer than the wood next to it.

- **Do NOT use a tack cloth to wipe down the blade surface.** After a few unfortunate incidents followed by some online research, I have concluded that the fluid in the tack cloth, likely acetone although I am not sure, can lead to big problems with epoxy curing. I do use a soft brush and then a dry tightly woven cloth. Loose woven softer cloth will often get caught on a point or in the grain and leave behind threads.

- Use a brush to clean your paper. Certain papers seem to clog up more readily than others. Before you throw it away try brushing it, it can make quite a difference.

[7]

Fiberglassing

The wood blade, absent its fiberglass outer coat, is fairly weak. Even though the Gflex epoxy used to join the shaft, thin and big pieces together has strengthened the blade, it still flexes and may seem unlikely to be strong enough to use. It may not even look very good. Wait until you see and feel the effect of fiberglass and epoxy. The transformation from bland, bendy, flexible wood, to richly colored stiff paddle blade is amazing!

At this point you should be done sanding the blade on both sides. Be sure and clean off the work surface and your work area. You don't want a sudden breeze blowing into your garage and depositing fine wood dust onto your freshly wetted surface. **Do not** use a tack cloth to wipe the surface. The tack cloth can leave an acetone residue behind that can really mess with your epoxy. Painful experience has shown me this. Even your hand can leave oil on the surface that can cause adhesion problems. Use a brush or a dry paper towel and leave it at that. Any sawdust still on the surface is not a bad thing. Consider it as filler!

I prefer four ounce fiberglass cloth for paddle blades. It's been my experience that this weight of cloth has the right mix of strength and "drapability" for use on a paddle blade. There are many different weights of fiberglass cloth. Some weights are heavy enough to repair large boats. The heavier the cloth the more it resists bending and draping over the objects it overlies. There's really light weight cloth as well, for uses that I have not yet discovered. There are also different weaves of cloth. If this interests you, do a bit of research and see if one style or another offers an advantage that warrants using it. I order fiberglass cloth from CLC Boats and have happily used whatever style their default cloth comes in.

Take the cloth out and carefully spread it out on a smooth surface. It's been my experience that fiberglass cloth will catch on just about any point that it can find, including dry or chapped skin. So a clean smooth surface is best. A ping pong table works great as does that old standby - the kitchen counter. For reference sake, the quietwater kit provides a piece of four ounce cloth twenty four inches tall and fifty inches wide. This is ample cloth for four separate pieces. Two pieces for each paddle. One piece for each side of the blade. I cut the big piece in half and carefully fold up one of the pieces and put it away. Edge fraying happens all too easily, so keep the touches to the unused glass cloth to a minimum. The remaining piece I cut in half again, which leaves me with a piece of cloth for each side of the blade.

As you likely discovered while sanding, it is nice to have a vise on a workbench. The vise continues to be handy when fiberglassing. Put the shaft into the vise with power face up and gently clamp in a position such that the blade is level and flat and up off your work surface. I use a little torpedo level to make the blade as flat and level in as I can in all directions so the epoxy does not flow to one side after I have poured it out.

Figure 35: Closely Trim the Dry Fiberglass Cloth-Around the Edge of the Blade

Fiberglass is fairly easy to cut with normal fabric scissors. The edges fray easily and the weave is easy to mess up, so minimize handling as much as you can. I like to size the piece as close to the size of the blade as I can, with very little overhang. Shooting for one-quarter inch of overhang is good, but be careful, too much trimming can leave you with too narrow of a piece. Like wood, fiberglass is hard to add back on.

Cloth extending out beyond the blade edge gets heavy once it is wet and tends to "bend", which in turn "lifts" the cloth on the edge up off the blade surface. This introduces air under the cloth which looks white when the epoxy is dry, which you do not want! Once dry you can sand this down, but now you have removed most of the cloth and much of the strength. Just keep a steady patient hand and aim for a slender quarter inch overhang.

As you position the cloth over the blade make sure that there are no loose strands UNDER the main piece. This strand will also annoyingly show up once you apply the epoxy. I extend the cloth as far up the shaft as I can make look good, usually about five inches above the bend. This is a taste thing. No laws requiring a certain length up the shaft. I trim the cloth portion on the shaft as narrow as I can. Figure 35 is a picture I took before I was done trimming the cloth along the shaft. When I finished, the cloth draping the shaft was probably three-quarters of an inch narrower ON EACH SIDE relative to what you see in Figure 35.

Wetting cloth on the shaft and keeping it straight and neat and unfrayed and the epoxy not running down the sides of the shaft is tricky stuff, so no need to go crazy with cloth up the shaft. Remember, the ever handy wax paper can be positioned below the edges of the paddle blade to catch any epoxy runs or drips. Trim this cloth nice and close to the edge of the blade. I shoot for about a quarter inch of overhang. A couple small clamps on the far side may help prevent the cloth from moving while you are cutting.

Optional Decal

The next few paragraphs discuss applying an optional decal. Rice paper when wetted out with epoxy becomes nearly transparent. After some experimenting, I found rice paper that printed well with an ink jet and went transparent when I wetted it with MAS epoxy over the top of western red cedar. The quietwater kit comes with a decal of your design (you just need to mail me the design). In the true spirit of DIYing, if this interests you, you can track down a rice paper source and go about this from scratch as well. I found the rice paper at a bookstore in the art supply section.

The next few paragraphs mix in applying the decal and then go straight into adding epoxy over the cloth. If no decal, just read through this section and don't worry about the decal bits.

If you have a rice paper custom decal and you want to apply it on the power face, get that out and lay it in position (decal can also go on back side if you want). The decal is printed in reverse. Lay it down on the blade with ink side against wood, such that when you look down on it, it reads normally (left to right; top to bottom) and not "backwards". Make sure it is right side up as well! This will put the ink side of the paper down against the blade. The paper will be "above" or on top of the ink. Easier to see than describe. See Figure 36. Look down on this before things get permanent and make sure you can read the decal. Trim as much of the non-inked paper away as you can.

Time to mix a small batch of the MAS epoxy. Do not use the GFlex for this blade work! If you have a kit, the epoxy you want to use comes in the blue and red tipped bottles. The blue tip is the resin and the red tip is the hardener. If you have a kit, replace the shipping tops of both bottles with the pouring tips. On first use you will need to cut the tips off of each pouring tip. Don't cut too much off the tip or the tip cap will not fit over the cut end. Again with the kit (MAS), you use two parts of the blue bottle (resin) for each one part of the red bottle (hardener)!

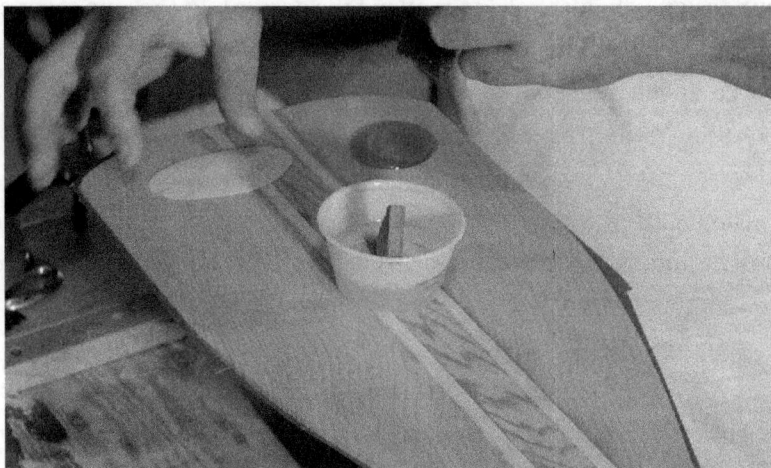

Figure 36: Decal and Epoxy Pool; Note the Blue and Red Lines on the Cup

Use one of the large mixing cups provided in the kit for this first batch of blade epoxy. The bottom of a paper coffee cup works well too. This batch will be about one and a half tablespoons. I like to go into the kitchen and use a kitchen tablespoon to pour one tablespoon of water into the mixing cup. I make a blue mark on the side of the cup so I know how much resin to add. Next I then use the ½ tbsp spoon to add that much more into the cup and then make a red mark at that level. Now I can easily maintain that 2:1 ratio of resin to hardener. Just use the marks when pouring out the resin and hardener. Be sure and get your eye down and look level at the marks as you squirt the liquid into the cup.

Stir the resin and hardener together to mix them up. Stirring can add bubbles to the epoxy, so stir slowly, no need to be aggressive here. I try and avoid bubbles in the epoxy whenever I can.

Pour a small pool onto the blade surface in the middle of where you want the decal. Spread this small pool out until it is about the size of the decal. Add small pours if necessary and push it around with the foam brush until it is big enough to immerse the decal. Carefully lay the decal down in this wetted area, ink side down, so that it reads/looks normal when viewed from above. Lay it down starting from one side, this lessens the problem of air bubbles getting trapped under the paper. Use the foam brush and firmly pat the decal down into the epoxy until it is saturated and you feel it make contact with the wood. You should feel it "sink" into the epoxy as you push it. The paper tends to float on top of the epoxy so firm but gentle pushing ensures that the paper is on the wood surface. No need to overdo this. The paper being on top of the ink acts to protect the ink from being smeared and running as you work the epoxy into the cloth overlying it in the next step.

Once you have the decal down and wetted in place, you are done with the decal.

Now immediately lay the cloth down over the top of this wet decal and quickly adjust it before the cloth starts to stick to the decal area. Pour any remaining epoxy across the top of the cloth. There likely will not be enough, so just mix up another small batch. No need to panic. Assuming you used the MAS in the kit, you have about a half hour before any appreciable hardening occurs. Regardless of brand, "pot time" is a common parameter in the epoxy world, just check that pot time and this is how much time you have to work the epoxy before curing really takes off.

Move your head around and look at this freshly wetted surface from a variety of positions. The goal is to see none of the weave and no obvious pooling of excess epoxy. Different positions can show you a run or a dry spot or a bit of cloth weave that can use more epoxy. If you see any weave or a dry looking spot, pout a tiny bit on the dry area and push it around until the weave has soaked up the epoxy and gone clear. Any excess epoxy will now pool on top and look "different", which ultimately means more sanding, so do not overdo it! Get your eye on all sides and use light from different angles to check and make sure you have nicely covered the entire blade surface. If you are seeing bubbles, they can be popped with a pin or a wood scrap or the edge of the brush.

In my experience, with this first pour it is better to be on the dry side and add additional smaller batches than it is to pour a large first batch and have the excess epoxy form "pools" on top of the cloth. The ideal amount of epoxy saturates the cloth and makes the weave texture disappear. Beyond that you start to see the epoxy pooling up on top of the cloth. I like using small foam brushes (if you have a quietwater kit, they are included) like little bulldozers to **SLOWLY** push the epoxy across the blade. Slow brush movements keep air bubbles to a minimum. Have a look at the surface from several directions, you will be able to see both drier weave areas and "overwet" pools where there is excess epoxy, just use the brush to doze this excess and spread it out.

Give this first coat on this first surface time to start curing. I do add a second lighter coat of epoxy, but I want to give the first coat time to begin curing, (but not completely cure) before I add the second coat. About forty minutes after the final pour of that first coat, I start checking the surface. To check the curing, I gently press a finger tip onto the surface. If my finger leaves a mark on the epoxy surface AND my fingertip comes away feeling dry and NOT sticky, that is the time for a second smaller batch of epoxy to be poured and spread on the surface of that first coat. If my finger leaves the mark AND feels sticky/wet, the first coat has not sufficiently cured. Continue checking every couple minutes or so, until your finger leaves a mark but comes away dry and not sticky.

At the point in the drying process, where your finger leaves a mark but comes away dry, you can still get chemical bonding to occur between the coats, ensuring good cohesion. It's still the same MAS epoxy for the second coat with the 2:1 ratio of resin to hardener, but you might make a batch about half the size of the first one, since the cloth is now saturated and will not soak up nearly as much fluid. Just pour out this second batch and evenly push it around. Nice and slow. If any cloth weave has become visible due to curing, make sure those "drier" spots get extra attention. No need to leave an epoxy "pool" sitting on the surface though, this is overkill and leads to more sanding. Leftover epoxy from this second batch can be applied up the shaft.

In my experience, more is NOT better with this second coat. I make it light. A good first coat that saturates the weave is going to give most of the strength. A light second coat fills in and could be considered mostly cosmetic, but still with enough benefit to warrant this second coat. For me, a heavy second coat and additional coats thereafter, add weight to the blade and no discernible benefit. Extra coats add weight, they are expensive and a good chunk of it could end up as dust. However, there is no law against adding extra coats. It is your paddle, so if you want a heavy second coat or even a third coat, go ahead and add it. Odds are it will not hurt anything nor will it likely help anything. Note that weight on the blade is weight you will notice more than weight anywhere else on the paddle.

The edges and bottom of the blade do not get covered with cloth. Cloth is not meant to bend at right angles, not even four ounce cloth, so there is no easy way to cover the edges. However, with cloth on both sides, the edge is almost certain to get a fair amount of epoxy on it while the epoxy is being spread. In fact, I stress more about epoxy running over the edge and wetting the underside of the blade and drying that way. So do check the underside and gently wipe away any epoxy you may see drying on the underside. While doing that simply rub the excess along the blade edges. Do not jiggle the wet cloth as you do this! Once both sides are covered and trimmed and dry, if you see dry spots on the edges, you can mix a tiny batch of epoxy and brush it on to the edges for another covering layer as well.

If the first coat completely dries prior to the second coat, you will need to sand the first coat surface before you apply the second. Sometimes this is the preferred route if the first coat surface is not making you happy.

Once you have a nice looking wetted surface with the second coat, you're done! Let this side dry. I like overnight. Give it some time. If this is the first side of your first paddle, be accepting of the results. **Every step of the way in paddle making gets better the more you do it!**

Once the first side is dry, take it out of the vise, pick it up and admire your work! The change from flexible, bendy piece of wood to something much stiffer and more richly colored has now started. Full curing can take a few days, so I hold off sanding this first side. Also if I sand now, there will be dust in my work space which I will need to clean (which I do not like) before I fiberglass the second side. So let the sanding wait until the second side is done and both sides have cured a day or so.

Use your fingertips to feel for high and low points on the surface of the blade. Do not expect perfect flat. This is not a machined surface, nor did a machine do the work. It's wood and you did the work. It's an organic surface. This touch test will give you a feel for where and how much you might want to sand. Again though, hold off until the second side is done before any sanding.

I use a sharp edge (old school razor blade is my favorite) and closely trim the dried fiberglass around the entire edge of the blade on this first side. This is another reason I like the 4 ox weight, it is fairly easy to cut. Heavier weights are harder to cut. I also check the under side and see if any epoxy made its way to the underside and dried. No sanding to speak of yet on that back face. If some epoxy worked its way under and onto the second side I do remove that, with sanding as needed.

After the finger feel test, an edge trim, and any sanding of dried drips on the back side, it is time to fiberglass the back side.

The second side is nearly a repeat of the first. Again, ideally using a vise, with the back side now facing up and as level as I can make it, I drape the second piece of fiberglass over the blade and trim it close to the edge of the blade. The tapered shaft is an issue on this back side. It is hard to get wet fiberglass to conform to this compound irregular shape. So with the dry cloth in its final resting place I cut a "notch" out of the cloth exposing the tapered portion of the shaft and leaving it uncovered. I make sure to get the cut edges of the cloth flat on the blade surface and in as close to the edge of the shaft along this notch as I can. I start out pouring the epoxy on the cloth right next to the shaft so that I can gently nudge the cloth up tight against the side wall of the shaft. The epoxy holds it in place. After this area is started then I pour the rest of the epoxy on the rest of the blade and start working everything around. Work it gently so as not to pull the epoxy away from the edge of the shaft. See Figure 37.

As on the other side, let this first coat dry until you can leave a fingerprint on the surface, but no epoxy adheres to your skin. Once your fingertip comes away dry, then pour out a smaller second coat and spread that. Avoid pooling the epoxy as best you can. Try to use reflected light to find the "light" areas where you might still see the weave, and make sure this second coat covers the light area.

Any extra epoxy left over after this second coat, I usually apply to the shaft. Light coats. The shaft is usually at an angle, so epoxy, if applied too heavily on the shaft, tends to run, which leads to more sanding. Light coats don't run. As much.

Once the second coat on this second side is dry, review your work and trim as needed. Now is the time to sand both sides. If the finger feel test turns up only minor areas, I start sanding with 150 grit, and move to 180 grit. 100 is very aggressive. 120 grit is also aggressive. Both can easily leave big scratches in the surface. 150 is a nice grit to start with, assuming all went well and you have a nice surface to start on. It's been my experience that it is very easy to sand through the epoxy and into the cloth fibers with 80, and 100 grit, so be careful with these grits if you choose to use them.

Cleaning the paper with a brush will prolong the life of each piece of paper and will increase the effectiveness of the sanding effort. Fiberglass dust quickly clogs the paper, so frequent brushing helps. You can also brush and wipe the surface of the blade. I think brushing and wiping the blade surface is better than blowing, which seems to get more of this nasty dust in the air where you might breathe it.

The goal with sanding is not a mass removal of dried epoxy. Keep in mind the more you remove the more you weaken this strength providing layer.

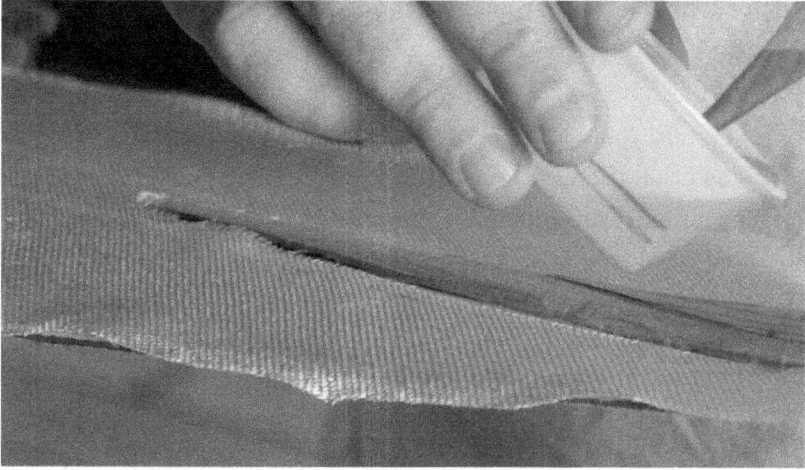

Figure 37: starting the epoxy on blade with notch cut out of fiberglass for taper

I like using fingertips to hold the sandpaper. The blade is an organic surface, so it may not be completely perfectly flat. Your fingers will feel this and help even out the sanding across the entire surface in a uniform manner. Using a block tends to overdo the high spots and underdo the low spots.

Before you get upset about a less-than-perfectly-flat surface, step back and think this through, before you get out the heavy artillery and start grinding out a flat surface.

Does the blade need to be perfectly flat? No.

Will this blade somehow be less efficient?

Why are you worried about efficiency? Paddling is pleasure. Efficiency is a work metric. Don't measure your pleasure. Enjoy it!

On a more serious note, I do not believe your paddling efficiency is impaired with an imperfect blade. Yes there may be cavitation on some tiny scale due to this less than perfect surface. But so what?

In my time paddling, I've never really felt that any of the blade surfaces I used were better or worse than other blade surfaces. I've noticed handle shape and shaft length more than blade surface. Worst case, if you perceive an issue with the blade surfaces of th is first paddle, apply what you have learned to your next paddle!

If I am in your shoes, I go for a nice, LIGHT, even sanding, which will cloud the surface by the way. I go through my paper progressions ending with the 220 grit and make sure that I do not see any swirls or other obvious sanding lines. No need for heavy downward pressure on the sandpaper. Remember that "Zen" thing. Let the grit do the work, lightly guided by your hand. Be careful sanding on the center shaft piece. Experiment with the amount of pressure until you feel comfortable with pressure versus results.

A coat of spar varnish restores the surface. A second coat of varnish even more so and I am done.

OPTION ASIDE – It is reasonable to wonder if leaving fiberglass off the tapered portion of the shaft will lead to a weakened piece of the paddle. So far, this has not been a factor in my personal paddles. In addition, the paddling movement is compressing this back side, non-power face, so the "bare" wood is being "squeezed" or pushed together rather than stretched apart.

If you feel strongly about this, save the notch piece you cut out and apply it over the tapered section of the shaft as best you can. Cutting gussets will help the cloth conform to this irregularly shaped piece of the shaft. I don't do this, having had no problems with this area so far and having had plenty of problems getting cloth to drape over the tapers. **END ASIDE**

[8]

Final Coating

For the finish there are several options available. Other than the epoxy itself, spar varnish is my first choice. But other options are out there. One parameter worth noting is that each finish feels different on skin and specifically may be quite different in feel when the surface is wet. You may or may not like how a finish feels when it is wet. Various oils, for example, come to mind, but matte, semi-gloss, and gloss varnishes can also be distinctly different. As I write this I must confess that having not worked with oils, I am uncertain about how an oil finish feels when wet. I also am uncertain about applying an oil over the top of epoxy on the blade. Seems to me this is likely not compatible. Google is wonderful, as are numerous woodworking forums when it comes to reading what others say about things like "wet feel" of a particular finish.

If you want to go beyond using epoxy as a finish on the shaft and handle, I like spar varnish. It looks good and protects the wood surface. There are many other finishing options that can be found via talking with other paddlers or a search engine to further inform your choice. For me, I like simple, so it is sand the epoxy, apply a coat of spar varnish, sand with 220 (maybe 180 if I have to) apply a light second coat let dry and go paddling. The simple quick finishes make it easy to not shed a tear WHEN (not if) that first nick, ding or gash happens.

If you are so inclined, the finish can be sanded between coats and multiple layers of finish can be added. Sand between coats with a 220 grit or finer. Lightly. Build up the finish as much as you want. No rules here. To your taste. Note that cool temperatures will slow down the drying time. It also seems to me that over the first three or four days the surface seems to steadily get harder. Again be patient. It is amazing what varnish and sanding can lead to given patience and repetition. It's not necessary for the function of your paddle, but it does protect the surface and it sure can look good.

The forum on the CLC Boats website is a great resource. If you are paddling in saltwater and/or if you are out under harsh sun quite a bit, a final finish with a UV protectant may be in order.

Keep in mind that wood paddles can be resanded and refinished as much or as little as you want. Remember that zealous sanding of the blade may bite into the fibers of the cloth, so don't overdo blade resanding, but you can certainly light sand and recoat to restore a final finish.

[9]

Conclusion

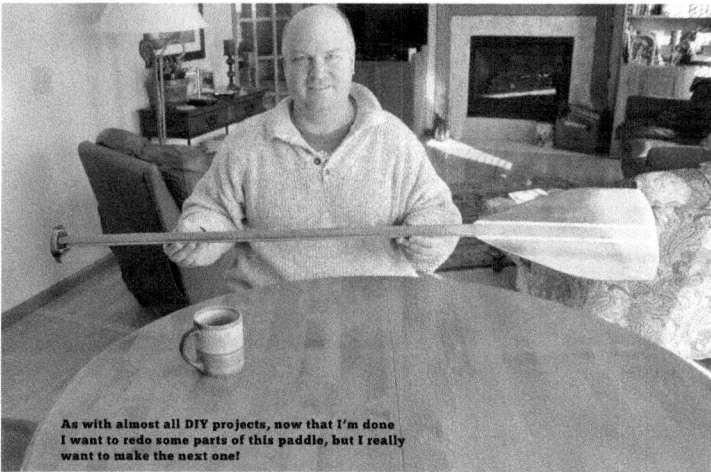

As with almost all DIY projects, now that I'm done I want to redo some parts of this paddle, but I really want to make the next one!

Figure 38: Finally it's you and a cup of coffee admiring your work.

And there you have it. One version of making a bent shaft laminated wood canoe paddle. I hope that your paddle making project is a satisfying experience. But if it was easy everyone would be doing it! So I expect that for at least some of you, the first paddle will lead to some frustration. Learn from those frustrations! Hand powered woodworking is all about experience. There's no other way to get it, other than doing it! With that in mind your first paddle experience should lead to a far better second paddle.

I think wood and hand tools fire up some dusty synapses in a more primitive part of our brain and lead to some very enjoyable time spent working with your wood instead of knitting in the living room and watching Sunday football. So good for you for getting out there and building your own paddle! Even more so if you involve your S.O. and/or your kid(s). Wood and hand tools have the same magic effect on both sexes and all ages!

I hope you continue building your own paddles and that you will consider calling or emailing me and ordering more of the materials for even more future paddling projects (hint hint). I will add updates, corrections, and new methods to the quietwater paddles website:
URL = www.quietwaterpaddles.com/updates.htm

May the splinters be few and the water continue to float your boat!

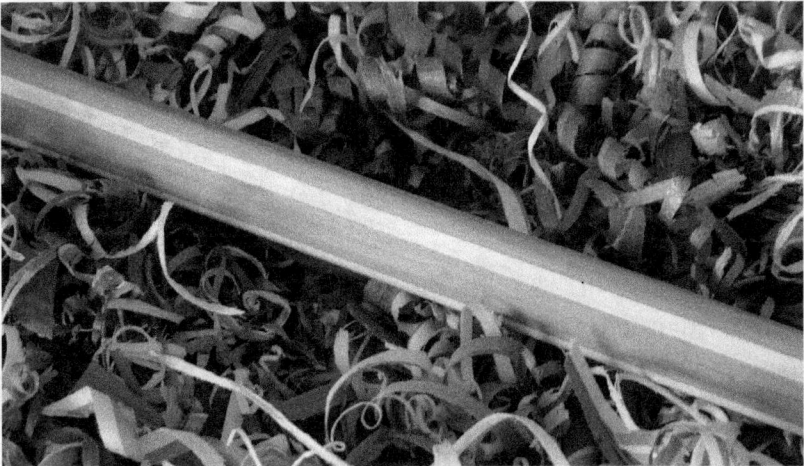

Jeff Bach – paddle@quietwaterpaddles.com

[10]

FAQs

"I found a typo OR I wish there was a picture that made x clearer."

I hope that you will let me know one way or another what you think about this book. I (Jeff Bach) can be reached at paddle@quietwaterpaddles.com. If you think that a particular step is confusing, send me an email with your question, because odds are that there are several people thinking the same thing. I will try and update the section and add an image to help clarify - you can check online for these updates and modifications from reader feedback, just go to- www.quietwaterpaddles.com/updates.htm

It's also worth noting that what I write and show in this book is merely what I have come up with. It may be that you can develop a better way. This is one of the many beauties of DIY!

"A wood shaft strip broke. What can I do?"

After the break step back. Ask yourself if you are forcing the wood a bit too much. Sometimes even if you are careful and gentle, things will break. Did the break happen along a line you can see? Anything is possible.

With the dry broken pieces, you need to make what boat builders call a scarf joint. This is simply a way to join two short pieces together to make a longer piece. Cut the broken ends off and set about making two ramps, one on each piece. The ramps are gradual, about eight time longer than the thickness of the piece. With the piece being 1/4-inch thick, the ramp needs to be approximately two inches long. The ramp on each piece provides the large surface area that the epoxy needs to create a strong connection. The ramps will slide against each other with epoxy on that sliding surface.

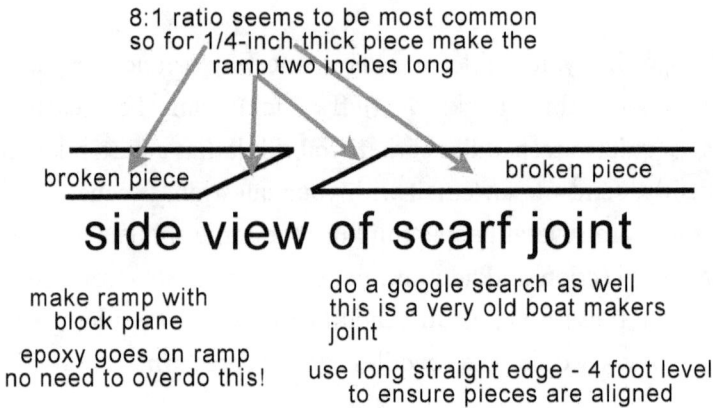

8:1 ratio seems to be most common so for 1/4-inch thick piece make the ramp two inches long

broken piece

broken piece

side view of scarf joint

make ramp with block plane

epoxy goes on ramp no need to overdo this!

do a google search as well this is a very old boat makers joint

use long straight edge - 4 foot level to ensure pieces are aligned

Figure 39: Possible Recovery from Break with a Scarf Joint

Once you have matching ramps cut, mix up a tiny bit of the GFlex epoxy (five drops each), coat the ramp surface and gently press the two ramps together. Be sure and put down wax paper under the work area, so the repaired piece does not stick to the work surface. Rub the surfaces around, get the air out. No void space in the bond is a good thing. Check for straightness. Sight down the length of it before and after adding a bit of top weight. It's easy to add a little kink at the break such that the short piece is at an angle to the long piece. Use a two or three foot straight-edge to (re)check your alignment, then put wax paper on top and put a small brick or five pound weight on top of the break and let it dry. Sight down the repaired piece as best you can to make sure the pieces are straight.

"My shaft pieces popped apart or came undone. Can I recover?"

Sometimes things happen. A phone call, kids, happy hour. It is all too possible that a mistake happens. When this occurs and your pieces pop apart, take them all the way apart as best you can and let them dry for a day. Come back a day later with your scrapers and work the dried epoxy. Scrapers do a marvelous job removing epoxy. Usually well enough that you can reuse your two pieces and simply redo the epoxy join. I really like the GFlex epoxy for joining wood. I'm sure there are other epoxies that are out there that also do just fine, it's just that I've been so happy with GFlex I have not used any other epoxy for wood joinery in paddle making, so I can not speak from experience with other brands.

"Can you do the joinery with multiple pieces at a time?"

Sure. But why the hurry? You can do it however you want, but spreading epoxy over multiple strips and keeping everything aligned is hard. Your hands get sticky, you knock the epoxy cup over, the wood spreader is messy, the epoxy starts to cure. One joint at a time is easiest and leads to best quality. It is hard if you are impatient though. Making a paddle is like therapy for the impatient.

For the paddles I have built on the kitchen counter, I do the epoxy joinery at night. It dries overnight while we're all sleeping. I make sure I am the first one up in the morning so I can move it off the counter and out of the way before anyone else is in the kitchen.

"My shaft strips are a bit warped! What can I do?"

I pack them tightly and pay attention to straightness but beyond that things are out of my control. Once you are assembling the shaft, the alignment bars pretty much force the strips into position. You can move the alignment bars to a different set of grooves nearer the apex of the warp. You can also add other bars to force the warp straight while the epoxy dries. Clamps and shims can come in handy here.

If a strip is warped and its bothering you, you can try running a damp rag along it on all sides, put it on edge, lay a weight on the apex of the curve and let it relax/dry in that position. Increasing the water content and then having it dry back out in a straight position **may** help straighten a warp.

"How do I hold the paddle while I am shaping the shaft?"

Depending on your workshop setup, holding the paddle while you shape it may be your biggest challenge. A workbench with a vise made for wood is ideal I take the metal "jaw" pieces off and replace them with wood pieces. The metal jaw pieces easily bite into the wood and leave permanent marks. Wood jaws not so much. See Figure 40.

Vises are surprisingly cheap. You do not need anything fancy, in fact it looks to me like the lower end vises are the ones with the easy to remove metal pads, that you need to replace with wood pads. I mounted my vise on a piece of 2x6. In turn I then clamp that piece of 2x6 onto my bench. I like the portability this allows. Sometimes I need the whole surface of my bench or countertop. With a vise setup like this, it is easy to take it down and free the whole surface.

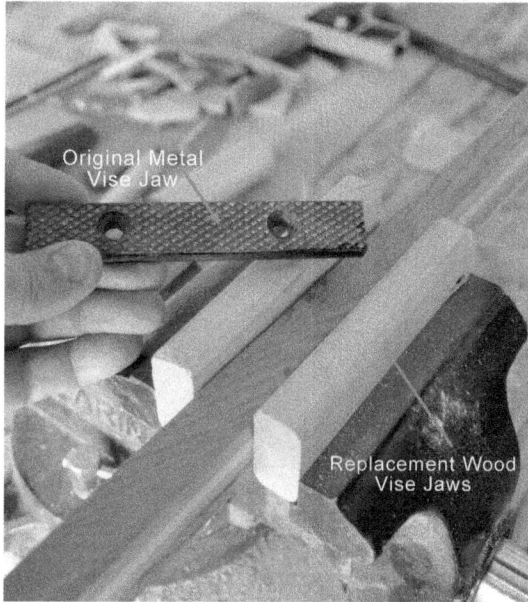

Figure 40: original metal vise and new wood replacements

Tables tend to move around a bit with a vise clamped to it. Countertops seem to be more solid. Be sure and use something under the 2x6, so the surface is not scratched. It could also be that when your S.O. is gone for the day, you bring in your vise mounted on the 2x6 and clamp it to the counter (with something underneath it of course). Do your work on this temporary arrangement and then five minutes before the S.O gets home you quick take it down and clean up. No one but you will be the wiser, although the S.O. may ask about the wonderful cedar smell.

Short of a vise, a couple pieces of wood and several clamps can suffice for the more creatively inclined. Clamp one piece down on the table or counter top. Lay the paddle shaft next to it. Lay the second piece down on the other side of the shaft. Use a couple clamps to squeeze the wood pieces together and a couple more clamps to secure the wood pieces to the table or counter.

OR lay the paddle down on its side. Put a wood piece over the top. Clamp down on the wood piece squeezing the paddle shaft between table and wood. Rube Goldberg lives!

[11]

Appendix 1 Form Plan

FORM BASE PIECE

The base of the form is a straight piece of wood. I use engineered wood consisting of several plies laminated together, rather than the usual one piece of wood cut from a tree. The pieces come in eight or nine foot lengths. I cut the piece in half, so the form base is either four or four and half feet long. I use engineered wood in lieu of a 2x4 or 2x6 because "normal" wood can warp. However if you have a straight 2x4 or 2x6 and you trust it, go ahead and use it.

The wood strips (laminates) that I use to make the shaft are one inch wide. This means you want the work surface of the form to be one inch wide. I make it a fat one inch to allow for the layer of wax paper I use to cover the surface. To achieve this work surface width, measure the total width of your base piece and subtract a fat inch. Divide the remaining amount by two. That number is the depth of a groove you must make on **EACH** side of the form with either a router or a table saw. Cutting grooves every ten inches on your form gives you some flexibility to move alignment bars around depending on where your shaft strips may be warped. Make the grooves in pairs, such that each groove is in line and right across from the groove on the other side. See Figure 41.

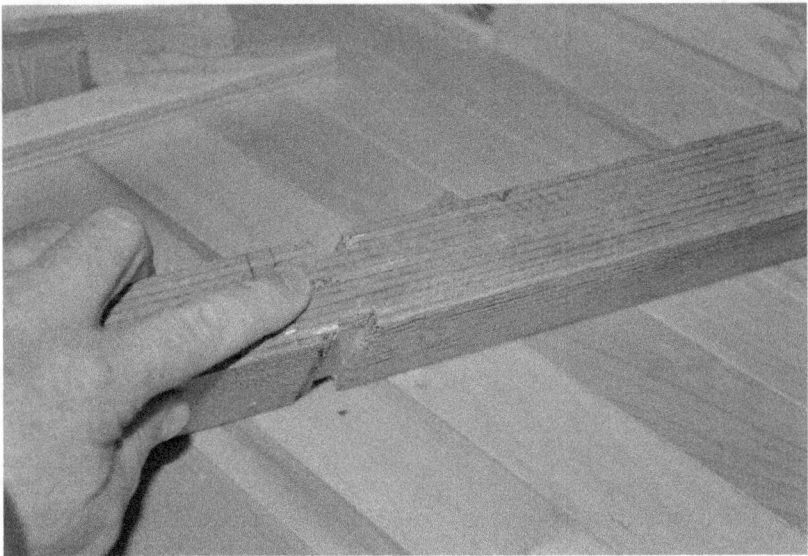

Figure 41: Paired Grooves

Alignment Bars

Into each groove you will place an alignment bar. The alignment bar is just a simple piece of wood the same width as the groove and approximately the same thickness as the depth of the groove. I make each bar about six inches tall. The bar fits in the full height of the groove and sticks up another two or so inches which is needed to align the shaft strips, which is what you are really after with these bars. I pre-drill one hole in each bar and counter sink it, so the one screw I use to fasten it in the groove does not split the bar when I am driving it. See Figure 42.

Figure 42: Alignment Bar in a Groove

Clamps

Once again a picture is worth a thousand words. Each clamp starts with two pieces of all thread. This all thread can be any size, although I find quarter inch or smaller easier to work with. The all thread needs to be cut into six inch pieces. Clean each cut and make sure you can thread a nut over the cut. All of the washers and nuts need to fit this all thread so be sure and buy it all in the same size and thread density. Each clamp also has two bases and one cross piece, four nuts that match the all thread, two wingnuts, a large fender washer and a normal washer. For the base piece I use scrap three-quarter inch plywood, so each base piece is 3/4-inch thick, 3/4-inch tall and three inches long. I drill and counter sink two holes for securing the base piece to the form. You will also need to pre-drill a hole for the all thread piece. So be sure and pick up a bit that matches the all thread. See Figure 43.

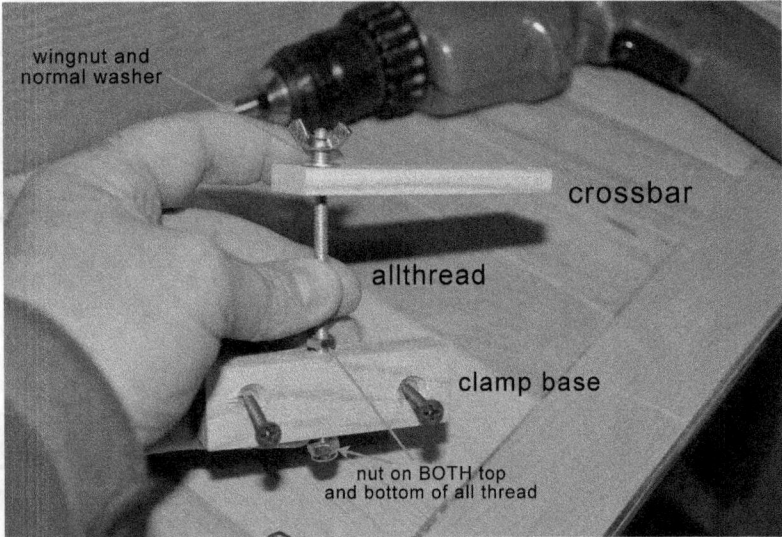

Figure 43: One Side of a Clamp Assembly; Other Side is just Base and Allthread

The cross bar at the top has a hole on one side and is then fit down over the all thread. A wingnut and normal washer secures it on that side. Do not cut the notch at this point. The other side is just the base piece and the all thread. Install both pieces across from each other. Once both bases are installed then close the cross bar and observe where it hits the second piece of all thread. Cut your notch such that it lines up and fits the all thread when you swing the crossbar closed. A wingnut and a large fender washer go on this side. The large fender washer distributes the force across this notch area.

Angle Block

The angle block is the next piece of the form. I use a 12-inch long piece of wood, usually a 2x4. There are simple angle measuring/layout tools available for measuring the 12 degree angle. As a woodworker you likely already know the issue with making an angled cut. You will need some sort of tapering jig to hold the wood piece as you make this cut on your table saw. I think the bed should be nice and smooth and flat which a table saw will provide. You could make this cut with a band saw, but I think you would be adding a rougher surface. I think it safe to write that the precision of the angle will depend on the saw and the jig you use to hold the wood as you make the cut. Don't sweat making this precise. An angle like this can be hard to layout, depending on the wood you use and your tools. In my experience +/- a degree or two is not going to end the world, nor has it affected my paddling pleasure. If you want to increase the angle (e.g. for your second paddle), you can simply add a shim between the form and the base of the angle block and add a few degrees to the bend in that manner.

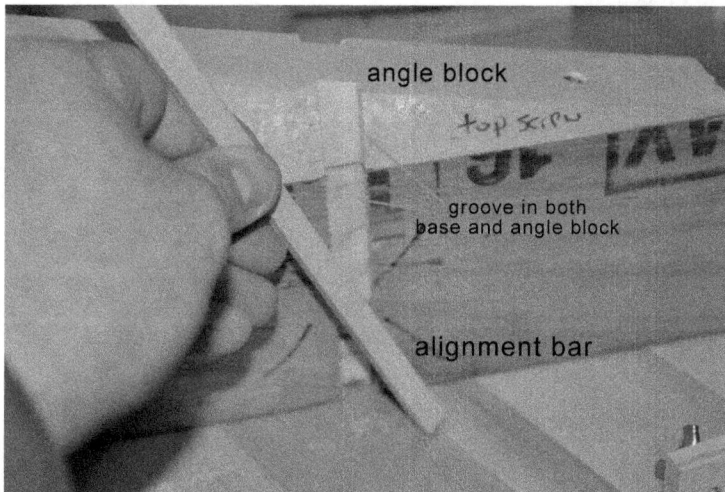

Figure 44: Angle Block, Groove and Alignment Bar

As you can see in Figure 44, I cut a groove into both sides of the angle block and use a pair of alignment bars to hold it in place. The alignment bars of course also serve to hold the shaft piece in line as it lies on the angle block. You can also optionally use a small wood screw to attach the angle block to the form base. I pre-drill and counter sink the hole for the screw as it is in the thin part of the block and may split the wood.

MATERIAL LIST

Other than the base of the form, the pieces are small and can be made from scrap wood you might have laying around. Dimensions are not critical, a clamp piece can be two inches and not three, the bars can be quarter inch and not three eighths. The world will not end if you vary the size. The list below is for a form with three clamps. If you want to add a fourth clamp, just buy some extra of the metal pieces. Without any further ado, here's the list of parts and pieces you'll need to make your own form:

Wood Pieces

- form base (s/b four feet long at least)
- alignment bars
- clamp base pieces
- clamp cross bar piece
- twelve inch piece of 2x4

Metal Pieces

- four feet of all thread (smallish diameter) &matching bit!
- three large fender washers (fits the all thread)
- three normal washers (fits the all thread)
- six wingnuts (fits the all thread)
- nuts (fits the all thread)
- a dozen small one-inch long wood screws

For tools, you'll need either a router or a table saw to make the matching grooves on the form. You will need a drill to make the holes for the compression block long bolts and to countersink the anchor holes for the compression blocks. You will need a hacksaw to cut the all thread into six inch long pieces and a metal file to clean up the cut ends, so you can run a nut over the cut. Finally a screwdriver for the screws or a screw bit for our drill.

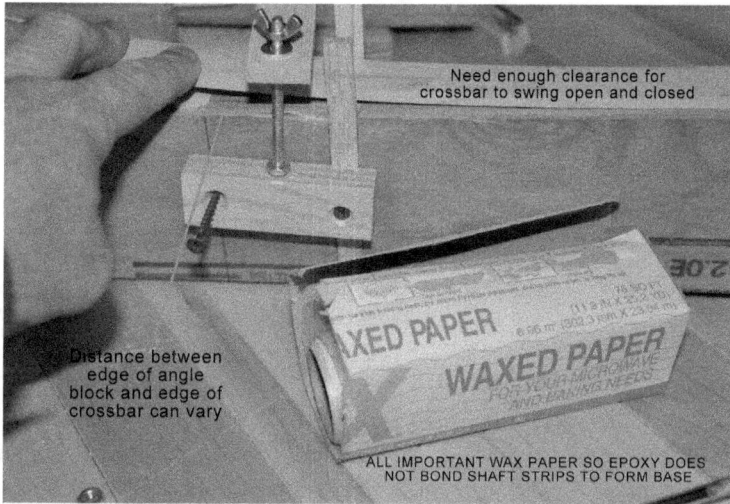

- Need enough clearance for crossbar to swing open and closed
- Distance between edge of angle block and edge of crossbar can vary
- ALL IMPORTANT WAX PAPER SO EPOXY DOES NOT BOND SHAFT STRIPS TO FORM BASE
- XED PAPER / WAXED PAPER

Figure 45: Clamp in place with angle block and alignment bars

ASSEMBLING THE PADDLE FORM

The form pretty much comes together as you make each component. Figure 46 shows two paddle forms from quietwater kits. Note the distance between the angle block and the first pair of bars. Also note the compression block location in between the angle block and alignment bar, with enough clearance for the compression cross bar to swing open and closed.

If in the heat of assembling your shaft pieces, you discover you do not like where a compression block pair is located, simply unscrew the base pieces and move the compression block to a better spot.

Figure 46: Canoe Paddle Forms Almost Ready for Use!

In Figure 46 please note the notch cut in the cross bar piece. This allows you to swing the clamp open and closed across the top of the shaft stack. The notch weakens the wood, so using a large fender washer on top helps distribute the pressure across the notch.

The form is straight, the cuts are uniform, the alignment bars are identical. In this way you make the form as straight and uniform as possible so that when you are laminating the wood strips they are all held in a uniform straight position while the epoxy dries. Be sure and use your eye to sight down the length of the shaft strips, and the form. Your eye is pretty good at spotting any warps or bows.

[12]

Appendix 2 Wood Pieces

Shaft Pieces

The paddles and kits from quietwater are made out of western red cedar, poplar, and trim pieces of various exotic woods. Each shaft is made up of five pieces of wood. Quietwater sells kits with the strips cut and ready to go. Enough for two paddles. However, if you have the table saw, the rip fence, the support stand, dust collection AND you can find vertical grain, clear cedar then go ahead and rip your own wood strips! I like a one inch wide wood strip that is one-quarter inch thick (that is what quietwater sells hint hint).

This book obviously does not come with the wood included. I personally like cedar and aspen. But there are many other wood species available. If you have other wood ready to go, feel free to use what you have on hand. At least for the first paddle.

I use clear vertical grain cedar for the shaft pieces. Both aspen and cedar have proven to be flexible enough to accept a bend. The lumber I buy comes in various widths and lengths. It does come in a true one inch thickness. This is the important dimension as the working surface of the form needs to match up with the true width of the shaft strips.

When I set up to do the ripping, I try and do the longest shaft piece and the blade pieces in the same session. It makes for easier finishing if the blade blanks and the shaft piece to which they are bonded are the same thickness. Cutting them all in the same session makes this matching thickness easier to achieve.

Strip thickness deserves a paragraph. I shoot for the shaft strips to be one-quarter inch thick and I set my rip fence accordingly. The quarter inch thickness works well for me with cedar and aspen when it comes to bending the shaft strips. Five strips x quarter inch gives me a shaft stack 1.25 inches "tall", which I have found to yield a nice finished size that fits the average hand. If you have big hands you can increase the thickness of each strip (say $9/32^{nds}$ or even $5/16^{ths}$; metric system is easier, too bad we don't use it!) if you want OR you could add a sixth strip.

Wood strips with an occasional knot may still be good enough for a wood paddle. Knot free is nice BUT if you have a couple small tight knots in an otherwise clear piece of vertical grain cedar, I think it is still worth using. Clear wood is expensive and you do pay for that clear piece. Knots are brittle. They tend to break rather than flex like clear wood does. Laminating wood strips together immensely increases the strength of the wood and somewhat covers up for the brittle knots. This MAY be enough to compensate for the weakness that the knot(s) may introduce. No guarantees, but if it was my piece of wood and small knots were present, I would make the paddle and enjoy its use as long as it lasted, expecting that it may break near one of the knots at some point.

vertical grain
western red cedar

Figure 47: Look for Clear Vertical Grain Wood Pieces to Rip for the Shaft Pieces

If vertical grain western red cedar is not available or you have something else in mind go for it. While western red cedar has a great history in small boating and a superb strength to weight ratio, there's no federal law I am aware of that requires its use. Pine, for example, is widely available. It's cheap. It might be hard to find knot free lengths. I've also found pine to be somewhat harder to work with. It seems to be a bit sappier and it can fight your tools a bit more. But pine is better than nothing by a long shot. So if that is what you have then use it.

THE SCARF JOINT

For the frugal lover of wood or the woodworker that has short pieces, a scarf joint is a method of joining short pieces or scrap into longer pieces. Done correctly, the scarf joint is as strong as a single piece of wood. It is an extra step, and there is a risk that the joint will be a differing stiffness than the wood above and below it. But again, if the other option is nothing, then using scarf joints to make short pieces long enough to use in a shaft strip is well worth the effort! See the FAQ section for more details on a scarf joint.

BLADE PIECES

If you have a table saw and a rip fence and assuming your idea for the blade matches what I show in the pictures, then you probably know that you can raise the blade, put your wood piece on edge and carefully push it through. On most table saws you can get a three inch tall cut. Much safer and easier to make two cuts with the blade set at about 1.75 inches. Be careful. Use a zero clearance plate on your table saw and push sticks. Or you could buy ready to use blade blanks from quietwater and avoid table saws altogether.

I try to rip the thin and the big blade pieces in the same session as the shaft strips. That way the fence does not change and neither should the thickness of those pieces. It's easier finishing if the thin blade piece (for me usually this is aspen) and the big blade piece are the same thickness as the shaft piece to which they are bonded.

You can vary the final width of your finished blade most easily by making the thin blade piece wider or eliminating it. The final width of the paddle blade is determined by the width of the shaft piece (one inch) + two thin pieces + two big pieces. I make the big blade pieces about three inches wide at the widest point. The thin pieces in a kit come in at about $3/8^{ths}$ of an inch wide. But if you are doing your own you can make them as wide as you want!

You can of course stray from the blade design I like, which is my personal subjective "like", and do something different. Another common option is to lay out one inch wide strips and epoxy them together into a wide piece. When that piece is dry you trace out your blade shape and cut that shape out on a band saw. Cut that finished piece in half and epoxy each half onto the center shaft piece. The somewhat hidden down side to this style of blade assembling is that the epoxy lines are harder than the wood and can dull or even nick your block plane and spokeshave sharp edges.

THE HANDLE

The handle that quietwater sells as part of the kit is a complex piece of shaped wood. About sixteen different cuts, all done on a table saw and a band saw with unique custom-made jigs, go into the handle. I developed the handle jigs for safety reasons. It is dangerous to make cuts on short pieces of wood that already have other cut short surfaces. Short pieces are hard to securely hold and move past the saw blade. Jigs also greatly help with making repeatable cuts, giving you similarly shaped pieces of wood. With this book you are on your own for a handle, assuming you want to make one similar to what comes with the kit. With your own tools though, you are certainly free to come up with your own handle design and shape. The sky is the limit. Just be careful and use all applicable safety devices! Kickbacks, kickouts, jams – they all happen, they're all moving faster than you can move out of the way. Fast moving wood pieces really hurt. So too does a sharp table saw blade.

BE CAREFUL

ABOUT THE AUTHOR

I've been paddling awhile. Maybe the majority of my life. I started paddling and poling in small ponds around our house in about fifth grade using an old beater canoe someone had given my Dad. From the small ponds my brother and I would drag that old canoe to, I evolved to working for a summer at Camp duNord near Ely and then the next summer guiding in the Boundary Waters Canoe Area in northern Minnesota.

From there, I went to guide on the Rogue and Deschutes Rivers in Oregon and the upper Klamath in northern California. After that and most of all, I have been lucky enough to guide on my much loved Main Salmon and Middle Fork of the Salmon in Idaho. All of it has been paddle-powered or oar-powered and all of it has been on some of the finest water that I could ever have hoped to wet a paddle or oar.

Figure 48: Gorgeous white sand beach on the Salmon River in Idaho; only other place I have seen with beaches like this are the sandbars on the lower Wisconsin!

Figure 49: Dropping Through a Wavetrain on the Main Salmon in Idaho

Back in the day, my brother and I had to make our paddles for canoeing those ponds in the woods. They were all one-piece jobs, carved out of a pine 2x6 with an old drawknife that I think I may have run off with from my grandpa's garage. I can't quite remember the provenance of that old tool. Anyway, that old drawknife began a lifelong affair with woodworking that continues today. I have evolved to prefer a spokeshave in lieu of the old drawknife. As you can see in the picture below, the first paddles my brother and I made were quite tall, one piece and featured woodburned animal tracks. The paddle in my right hand must be about six and half feet tall. I vaguely remember reading quite a bit about the French Canadian voyageurs and their tall paddle and thin blades...

Figure 50: My Parents Saved My First Paddles from About Age
11; the Paddle in My Left Hand is the One I Made for the Book
and DVD

Paddling has also lent itself well to getting my family outdoors doing something together.

Figure 51: They're grown up now, but they were little then!

As in many other things, I find strength in paddle making is overrated. Finesse and technique win out more often than not. In the case of paddle making, strength does not come from where you might expect. For the shaft, strength comes from the laminating process, from joining weak individual pieces together into a much stronger group. For the blade, strength comes from the fiberglass and the epoxy. The underlying wood provides the good looks and the shape, but the fiberglass and epoxy do the heavy lifting. I am still surprised at how strong a soft, wimpy (but beautiful) wood like cedar becomes when you laminate it together.

Might be a life lesson in there somewhere.